KAREN RUSSELL

Sleep Donation

VINTAGE

1 3 5 7 9 10 8 6 4 2

Vintage is part of the Penguin Random House group of companies
whose addresses can be found at global.penguinrandomhouse.com

Penguin
Random House
UK

Copyright © Karen Russell 2014, 2020

Illustrations by ALE + ALE, copyright © 2020 by
Alessandro Lecis/Alessandra Panzeri

Book design by Debbie Glasserman

Karen Russell has asserted her right to be identified as the
author of this Work in accordance with the Copyright,
Designs and Patents Act 1988

First published in the UK by Vintage in 2020
First published in the United States by Vintage Books, a division of
Penguin Random House LLC, New York, and distributed in Canada
by Penguin Random House Canada Limited, Toronto
Originally published as an ebook by Atavist in 2014

penguin.co.uk/vintage

A CIP catalogue record for this book is available
from the British Library

ISBN 9781529111354

Printed and bound in Great Britain by Clays Ltd, Elcograf S.p.A.

Penguin Random House is committed to a sustainable future for
our business, our readers and our planet. This book is made
from Forest Stewardship Council® certified paper.

For Ada Starling Perez,
the best sleeper in our family

SLEEP DONATION

THE SLEEP VAN

The siren goes, and we code for dispatch. Nine times in twenty, lately, it's the same address: 3300 Cedar Ridge Parkway.

Then we get a call back, saying the dispatch is canceled.

Then we get a third call: no, disregard the cancellation; get a Sleep Van to the property, stat.

What's happening, as revealed to us by a visibly distraught Jim: Mr. and Mrs. Harkonnen are having a "dispute."

"Mr. Harkonnen says he wants to drop out."

"So what?" says the intern. "We don't even use his donations."

"No, jackass. He's trying to pull out with Baby A."

Everybody looks over at that.

Rudy slaps his bald spot and leaves his hand there. A grapefruit hue spills underneath his fingers, as if the scalp is blushing.

Jim freezes in the center of the trailer, in full view of every staffer, and rubs his fists against his gray eyes. It's a pitiful and futile gesture to witness, like watching an animal cower inside a plastic cage. We can see how scared Jim is of losing both things: Baby A and our good opinion of him.

Six staffers are working the phones tonight, and we are all mentally coaching him: *Don't cry, Jim.*

Our Sleep Station has an unusual, top-heavy hierarchy—we have two supervisors, the Storch brothers. They are former CEOs who left the business world at the height of the Insomnia Crisis to found the not-for-profit Slumber Corps and now freely give all their resources to its efforts. Money, time, intellect, leadership, creativity, toilet seats. The Storches made their fortune in the ergonomic toilet business. You may have seen their advertisements: "To shit upon a Storch feels better than a visit to your chiropractor." Their extreme altruism is a provocation to everyone else on staff—an inducement to work even harder, a reminder that we could always be giving more.

Rudy and Jim have been my supervisors for seven years; I was the first recruiter assigned to their team. I don't socialize with them outside work. Our contact is limited to this office (unless you count our public performances at Corps fundraisers, the charity balls and charity golf-offs). But I know every shadow of my bosses' faces, all their Storchy tics, that upsetting thing Rudy does with his pen caps, what Jim's not saying at our meetings. The brothers are middle-aged Irish twins, clean shaven and built like longshoremen. Externally, they have slate eyes and cranberry-red hair, balding in identical horseshoe patterns. Internally, each brother has his own uniquely fucked emotional metabolism. Rudy, for example, is currently managing his despair by bawling out the interns, sweat jeweling all along his dusky face like a July whisky glass.

The Storches are celebrities in the sleep crisis community. Eight years ago, the brothers served together as executive directors of the inaugural Slumber Corps Board at headquarters in Washington, DC. Within months, the Corps had established outposts in every major city, pullulating green offshoots of the DC base. Soon local branches began operating more or less independently, soliciting donations for money and sleep, whereupon the Storch brothers resigned from the board and promptly requested a demotion to this low-prestige placement in their home city. A Solar Zone assignment. They wanted to work directly on the front lines—to "embed" with us, according to Rudy, perhaps not the best choice of words during an insomnia epidemic. They claim to prefer our trailer to the DC offices. We serve an urban core where the rate of insomnia is twenty-two percent higher than the national average. Our Pennsylvania city has one of the greatest REM-sleep deficits on the East Coast (although we are certainly not the worst hit: Tampa, riddlingly, currently leads the nation in new cases of the insomnia; the governor's budget cuts in the Sunshine State have meant that Floridian sleep scientists remain stalled at the "dang"/"go figure" stage of their research). Hundreds of our old neighbors, friends, coworkers, and teachers are new insomniacs. They file for dream bankruptcy, appeal for Slumber Corps aid, wait to be approved for a sleep donor. It is a special kind of homelessness, says our mayor, to be evicted from your dreams. I believe our mayor is both genuinely concerned for his insomniac constituency and pandering to a powerfully desperate new voting block.

Currently the National Center for Environmental Health is investigating possible environmental causes in our city: everything from the water table to disturbed eagles' nests to the brilliance of the moon on grass to the antique screams of the historic monorail.

I grew up here, too.

We operate out of a Mobi-Office. Six interlocking trailers, dry-docked on a vacant downtown lot that the Corps leases from the city. "The labyrinth," Rudy calls it. A former FEMA engineer designed it as a temporary accommodation; a base camp for local teams working at the frontiers of the crisis. We've been working out of our tin can for half a decade. Nobody suggests moving into a brick-and-mortar office; nobody wants to peer through glass windows, in a building with a foundation, and admit that the insomnia emergency is now a permanent condition.

You'd think it would be difficult to hide in a trailer. But I'm chameleoned next to the phone wall, near the black window. Some intern has made curtains for the trailer windows, snaggy lace, that look nothing like curtains, in fact, but like vestments tiny and obscene: bridal veils for mice, chinchilla negligees. They flutter in the trailer's manic air-conditioning. Outside, the moon is a colossus. Its radiance makes every white of human manufacture seem dingy, impure.

I turn from the moon, remove the headset; I give myself one more blank moment.

"Where's Trish?"

"Get Trish."

"Over here," I say.

"Edgewater!" screams Rudy. "There you are! We have a major goddamn problem."

"A hitch," Jim soothes.

"The mother is solid; she's one hundred percent. The father, though—"

"The father is afflicted with doubts."

"The father is a selfish prick."

"Trish, honey . . ."

"Bastard hung up on me twice."

"Whose signature is on the consent? Do we have both?"

Now everyone is staring at me.

"We do," I say smoothly. "I have the file here."

"Edgewater will handle this," Rudy prophesies, staring right at me.

"Mr. Harkonnen needs to be reminded of why this is important."

"Life or death."

"I think he knows, Jim. I already pitched them."

"*Them*?"

"Her," I admit. "The mother."

"Aha!"

"But I'm sure she's told him about Dori—"

"Not the way *you* tell it, Edgewater." Rudy beams at me. Rudy is the kind of boss who goes from screaming to beaming in two seconds flat, at a psychopathic velocity.

"He's got to hear it from you. Face-to-face."

"Only a stone would refuse to donate after your pitch."

"Trish, baby."

"Edgewater."

Pride heats my eyes. It's reprehensible, but that's what happens.

"It might not work," I say. "If he's that dead set against it."

Jim and Rudy pour it on even thicker, emphasizing that I am indispensable to the organization, that the Corps would be lost without me, et cetera.

"Look at you!" Rudy grins.

"Look at those hands," Jim says approvingly.

We look at my hands, which are shaking. I feel proud again, which has got to be the wrong response to a set of involuntary tremors. My body knows what I'm about to do, and it's balking, just like Mr. Harkonnen.

"You are the genuine article, Trish."

"Okay."

"You are simply the—"

"I said I'll go, Rudy."

Rudy is a bad recruiter. I've seen him in action. Potential donors sway on the brink of a yes, prepared to surrender to the gravity of the appeal, but then Rudy gets overzealous, Rudy turns the solicitation into a game of coercion, until at last his lip-smacking anticipation of their gift makes them wary again, and they stiffen into a no.

"That's how we got Baby A, you know," Jim whispers to the intern, Sam Yoon, a college junior in a mint-green dress shirt who is earnestly frowning as I exit the trailer; it's a whisper I know I'm meant to hear.

"Trish pitched Mrs. Harkonnen at a Sleep Drive in a parking lot. Nabbed her right outside the grocery store, schlepping Baby A. Watch her pitch sometime. Shadow her at a drive. She's just pure appeal, pure passion for the cause. Her sister was Dori Edgewater."

"Oh my," says the intern, exactly matching Rudy's tone.

What distinguishes me as a recruiter, I'm told by Rudy and Jim, is that my sister's death is evergreen for me, a pure shock, the freshest outrage. I don't have to dig around with the needle; that vein is open on the surface.

"And Trish can't fake it."

"Cries every time."

"Quakes, like."

"She gets emotional, and people really respond."

"Describes the sister like she's standing right in front of her."

"Sobs like she's still at the wake—"

Jim frowns, self-startled.

He's a midsentence self-startler, Jim. "Hiccups of insight," he calls these moments. Whenever my boss is struck dumb by his own epiphanic inner light, I picture a tiny deer jolted out of its grazing with grass in its mouth, paralyzed by the brilliant approach of a Mack truck.

"Wait a sec, Rudy, why the hell do we call it that? A wake? For a dead gal? That's terrible. That's goddamn macabre."

"I've wondered that myself. Seems a pretty grim joke."

"Oh, there's definitely a reason," says the brown-nosing intern. "Some Catholic logic. Or is it a Jewish thing?"

"People respond!" bellows Rudy. "Edgewater, she's a little engine. Even our most resistant demographics will give to her. Males, retirees! Greenwich bankers, West Texas construction workers. The Southeast Asian community, where, as you well know, there is a culturally rooted suspicion of sleep donations."

"Of course." The intern nods.

"But they have no immunity to Edgewater's story."

I am hovering near the trailer door, holding my breath. They keep talking, and I listen. I desperately need what they are offering. A faith transfusion. The *why* and the *how* of the organization. Our work and its value.

. . .

In high school, the Red Cross blood truck would pull up behind the trailers to collect donations from young, hale students, who got to skip homeroom and eat a raisin cookie and relinquish pints of type O. Dori gave, but I never did—I convinced myself that I was scared of needles. If I'd known then that I'd wind up here, begging strangers for an hour of their sleep, I think I would have given blood at every opportunity.

As a Corps volunteer, my duties are numerous and varied. Weekends, I mobilize the Sleep Van—a moonlit enterprise that dispatches a volunteer team to the homes of good sleepers, who have signed up to donate their rest to insomniacs. A Sleep Van has a spartan interior. The beds we call "catch-cots." If the van is equipped for infants and children, it features catch-cribs and trundles. Nurses slip on the anesthetic mask, open the IV of special chemicals, relieving a donor of consciousness; next, they clamp on and adjust the silver helmet, which does chafe a bit; one to two minutes after the loss of consciousness, once the donor enters a state of artificially stimulated sleep, the draw commences. The air in the Sleep Van turns balmy as the tubing heats; a donor's dream-moist breath gets siphoned into nozzles that connect to our tanks. Healthy sleep is pumped out of the body into long, clear tubes.

Weeknights, I recruit.

We set up for Sleep Drives in neighborhoods across the county, right at sundown.

Nurses swab out helmets in multiple vans, preparing to take sleep donations for testing. Administrators sit inside lit tents on suburban lawns, holding clipboards, prescreening donors with an eligibility questionnaire to filter out those whose sleep is prone to nightmares, disturbance. We babble the questions to volunteers under the midnight pines.

"When was your last full night of deep, unbroken sleep, ma'am?"

"When did you last dream about barking dogs, outer space, red grass, an ex-wife? Now, please be honest, sir—if your sleep was disturbed by her face, check the box . . ."

. . .

For most of the twenty-first century, insomnia was treatable by prescription medicines; I can still remember going with my father to pick up my sister's sleeping tablets from the owl-faced pharmacist. Capsules of Silenor—half white and half carnation pink. Dori's sleep trouble began early, at age eleven. Back then, before the disease progressed, medications reliably put her under. I used to study my sister's face on the pillow, trying to catch the moment when the Silenor took effect.

Once her adolescent insomnia ratcheted up, for unknown reasons, into the full-blown disorder, Dori slept about four hours a night. But for years, this was enough. The body can be a marvel of resiliency, a cactus when it comes to sleep—capable of surviving on mere drops.

By twenty, however, Dori had developed a resistance to all sleep aids. She also became, quite suddenly, impossible to anesthetize. We learned this when she broke her leg in college and surgeons were forced to operate on a fully conscious Dori.

The anesthesiologist is still writing papers about her.

Her leg healed, but soon Dori lost the ability to sleep even three hours a night. She could not stay down long enough to cycle into REM. She had to drop out of college and move into a white hospital room. What didn't they try on her? Dexmedetomidine, propofol, sevoflurane, xenon. The tranq gun used to bring down zoo elephants would have stopped her heart, or I'm sure they would have given that a go. Nobody could shade or muzzle her mind.

For the next year and seven months, Dori barely slept. Then the loss became total. The final day of my sister's life unwound with zero regard for the moon or the sun. She died awake, after twenty days, eleven hours, and fourteen minutes without sleep. Locked flightlessly inside her skull.

As an adolescent, I used to seethe with jealousy, because whereas I got auburn stubs, Dori had these fringed butter-fly eyes, jet lashes that curled so outrageously around her Caribbean-green irises that strangers assumed they were drug-store falsies. During her endless Last Day, I remember studying those eyelashes pasted to her skin, at an angle of unrelieved attention. She blinked at me, her thinking slow as syrup, and I wished that she would not smile again, not ever again, not like that, because by that point every smile was an accident, a twitch driven by nothing that I recognized as human. My mouthy, gor-geous, stupid-brave sister Dori, Miss "Drive It Like You Stole It" (even when the only "It" available to us was our great-aunt's haunted house of a wood-paneled Chrysler—who ever heard of a car with termites?), Miss "Three Jobs, Two College Majors, *and* There's a Flask in My Purse" was at this point a nobody. A "vegetable," as they say—the doctors' potted plant. And I hated the sight of her facial muscles pumpkin-grinning on the pillow, her pale eyes twitching, and I hated watching her go speech-less under the conglomerate weight of so much unrelenting looking and thinking and listening and feeling, her mind worn thin by the sound of every cough and the plinking moisture of every raindrop, these noises exploding like grenades through her naked awareness—her mind crushed, in the end, by an ava-lanche of waking moments. Once sleep stopped melting time for Dori, she could not dig herself out. She was buried under snowflakes, minutes to hours to months.

The official cause of death was organ failure.

I know it doesn't sound like much, on paper.

The same month Dori died, the CDC released the first case definition of the new terminal insomnia. Early estimates suggested that several hundred people in the United States were suffering from a total sleep loss; one year after my sister's funeral, this number had swelled to twenty thousand. "Orexins," the media taught us to call them. So that, almost immediately, the disorder became a metonym for its chosen victims. George Washington University Hospital opened the first dedicated critical-care insomnia ward—it was full within days. Congress allocated two billion for research.

It was not long thereafter that the mechanics of sleep donation were refined by Gould's team at the DC sleep clinic, and the Slumber Corps began its good work.

In the months following the CDC release, many people dismissed the disorder as an exaggeration of a universal American condition. Who was sleeping enough? Nobody! The "crisis" seemed like more TV hyperbole designed to keep us glued to our screens, watching mattress commercials. America, in the childhood of our understanding of the insomnia crisis, called the first victims liars, hypochondriacs, wackos, crank-addicts, insurance defrauders, anxious plagiarists of "real," biological disorders.

Now, of course, we know all too well that the insomnia epidemic is real. You need only consult its victims' pink-spoked eyeballs, their gaunt faces engraved behind moonlit windows. Neuroscientists have since concluded that for a significant portion of the country's population, the signaling function of the neuropeptide orexin has become impaired. Orexin deficiency has been linked to human narcolepsy, but this dysfunction causes the opposite effect: an untenable hyperarousal. Sleep becomes impossible. People like Dori remain conscious for months and even years, hostages of their brain's chemicals, trapped in the vigilance state that eventually kills them.

What triggers the dysfunction in some brains as opposed to others? Do these people have some inherited anomaly—an underlying genetic predisposition to wakefulness? A higher-wattage consciousness? Or is the trigger environmental? Nobody knows. It's the two-billion-dollar question. To date, every known case of the orexin-disruption has occurred in the Americas; nobody knows why this should be so, either. Some speculate that the sickness is connected to the oceans' tides, magnetism, the poles, the hemispheres, the net of light and shadow on the globe.

Other pundits promise, with weird relish, that we are seeing "the end of sleep as we know it." TV has become a glum Hall of Prophets: Dr. Daveesha Frank from the Boston Sleep Tank, who speaks like a robot programmed to self-destruct; dour professors wearing sunflower-yellow ties that film well. According to these professional Cassandras, sleep has been chased off the globe by our twenty-four-hour news cycle, our polluted skies and crops and waterways, the bald eyeballs of our glowing devices. We Americans are sitting in an electric chair that we engineered. What becomes of our circadian rhythms, the "old, glad harmonies" that leaped through us like the vascular thrust of water through leaves of grass? Bummer news, Walt: that song's done. And the endogenous clock, the suprachiasmatic nucleus, hereditary prize of every human, the tiny star cluster of neurons in the hypothalamus that regulates our yawning appetites for hard winter light and spacey blackness, the master clock that syncs us to one another, and to the earth's rotation, to the sun and the moon? To all the sister kingdoms on the twenty-four-hour circuit? Bacteria, Gila monsters, great sequoias, blue whales, orange groves, bear cubs, mustangs, toadstools, leopards, golden eagles, hyacinths, hippopotamuses, those tiny wizards—the butterflies, those glue artists—the arachnids, and all the sequined life on the seafloor, the black urchins that improbably still clock time with us? Bummer news, everyone: The clock stops for humanity. Time as we conceive it will soon become an anachronism. Time, as our species has lived it on this planet, will cease to exist. No more dark/light binary. No more active red daytime, blue evening dissolving. No longer is sunshine the coagulant of consciousness, causing us to clot into personalities, to cohere once more on our pillows each morning. These TV scientists predict "a global desertification of dreams." Soon, they promise, the disruption will afflict all of us. Sleep will go extinct. And eventually, unless we can find some way to synthesize it, so will we.

Generally, I'm mistrustful of these warblers, who do the dread crescendo. But I'm embarrassed to report that the Slumber Corps has borrowed a page from their playbook, "eschatological manipulation." At Sleep Drives in Alabama, Georgia, and Florida, we are test-screening a documentary created by those ratings whores, the worst of the cable news fear lords, "Is Sleep Going Extinct?" I'm afraid to say it's been very effective. We show it at night, like a popcorn horror flick. Terror, we've discovered, is a powerful donation-stimulant.

Meanwhile, sleep clinics in this country are operating at two hundred percent capacity; Night Worlds have sprouted all over America. Night Worlds have some kinship with the circled wagon trains of the West: the sleepless closing ranks against the night. They form spontaneously, on the margins of cities, but have developed an oddly standard layout: mazes of tents, nocturnally blooming speakeasies. Night World merchants cater to the sleepless ones with black-market remedies: "moonlamps" to ease the dreariness of unremitting wakefulness, "cave medicines" derived from ancient myrtles and lichens. Songbirds from Germany and Thailand are sold as "biocures"—their binary chirping is said to reprogram dreams into the mind. Some Night Worlds function as quasi-legal campgrounds for homeless and unemployable insomniacs. These places are tolerated by the local authorities because they help the hospitals with overflow. At the ERs, many new insomniacs are being turned away nightly. Sent back to twist in exile on their mattresses, cutting their eyes on the moon's blade until a donor can be found for them. They await our call. Until they are eligible for a sleep donation, there is nothing to be done for the majority of these people.

At Sleep Drives, we also screen the now-infamous footage of one of the first cases of terminal insomnia: a young Guyanese woman from a suburb of Houston. After five weeks of near-total sleep loss, her braids have turned totally white. Her face is child-smooth. She presented at the Gould clinic in DC after fourteen complete days and nights without cycling into sleep. She is wearing a fluffy pink sweater, lilting gibberish. Her eyes bulge so that you cannot see the lids.

Nothing newsworthy, you might correctly assert, about the public performance of illness. Death's dress rehearsal is ongoing at any bus stop in America, where sick people beg us not for minutes of sleep but for metallic dollar-flakes, wealth dandruff. Long before the sleep crisis, our downtown was a maze of sidewalk asylums. Immobilized people form a human shrubbery behind the courthouse, their lips whispering, their pink and brown palms extended, flat fronds shivering with need. Which is all to say: nothing the least bit strange to us, about public psychosis.

What makes this footage harrowing is its juxtaposition with a photograph of this Guyanese woman taken just five months earlier, before the onset of her orexin-disruption: her hazel eyes were shining and calm, tenanted by a sane woman, tethered to her memories; the eyes were seeing, presumably, only what was visible to everyone else in the room; her face was happy and plump, irrigated by sleep.

The young Guyanese insomniac never slept another minute. Unbeknownst to her doctors at the time of filming, she had already entered her LD, the ultimate interval of wakefulness that precedes death. LD for Last Day was a new acronym then, midwifed into the language by the sleep crisis; today, it's universal med-slang. Kids of six use "LD-er" as a playground insult. Schools instruct children to treat orexins as "ordinary" humans (an instruction that contains its own defeat, doesn't it?). The video is now nine years old. We'll keep looping her forever, for donors. Twelve days after they shot her segment, she died. Her true name was then released to the public, like a genie unbottled: Carolina Belle Duncan, age nineteen. Today she is a CDC celebrity: the first recorded death from the orexin-impairment. Dori was the East Coast's inaugural mortality, the fourteenth recorded death nationally.

A Johns Hopkins neurologist claimed that a mere *two hours* of recovery sleep would have prevented Carolina's death from cardiac arrest. Nine to thirteen hours, he said, would have ended her hallucinations and readmitted her to the waking world with stable vital signs. The insomnia's worst effects could be undone that speedily. One night's sleep would have saved her life. He compared it to getting an emergency tank of oxygen to a stranded diver.

Nine to thirteen hours—that figure haunted me.

It haunted everybody, apparently.

Without sleep, how long can a person live? The record was set last year when a woman in Devil's Creek, Nebraska, collapsed after twenty-two days. Five hundred and twenty-eight hours, without a minute of replacement sleep. Masked like a raccoon, at half her original weight. Her body had rejected all transfusions. She was a white lady, but her face had turned a blotchy pale blue. Yet this is a deceptive figure: twenty-two days. Months before her death, the Devil's Creek woman had reported a complete cessation of sleep. Many insomniacs who claim they haven't slept a wink in years are, unwittingly, lying to us. Patients swear they are awake. But the EEGs show that regions of the brain are going off-line. Neuronal networks shut down, fire on again, in a sort of cortical round-robin. "Microsleeps." Rolling blackouts. Some areas go dark for whole minutes; still the insomniac claims to be fully awake. In effect, the brain doses itself with eyedroppers of unconsciousness. We think microsleep must account for certain orexins' surprising longevity; some LD-ers, like Dori, can hang on for weeks before death from cardiac arrest, stroke, multiple organ failure.

Since joining the Slumber Corps, I've become obsessed with statistics. For bedside reading, I'll sometimes turn to our brochures. I do a dozy arithmetic under the skirted blue lamp, until these numbers add up to a temporary conviction that I deserve a night's sleep.

- 18 Insomniacs Will Dream Tonight, Thanks to Your Gift.
- Less than 1% of donors experience any kind of adverse reaction.
- Since its inception, this branch of the Slumber Corps has helped over 3,000 insomniacs.
- There are close to 250,000 people currently on our waiting lists nationwide. Priority always goes to urgency of need.

And my favorite:

- 34% of Insomniacs Will Regain Their Natural Ability to Sleep after a SINGLE TRANSFUSION.

Our work really does save lives. Nobody can deny that extraordinary fact. During the early trials of the sleep-donation procedure, Gould's team made an astonishing finding. For roughly a third of patients, full recovery from the orexin-disorder is possible after a single ten-hour transfusion.

Doctors cannot yet account for why some patients continue to suffer from the orexin disruption and require multiple trans-fusions, whereas others are "reset," cured. The mode of action is unknown. Some doctors posit that, like an electroconvulsive therapy treatment, or electroshock therapy, a sleep transfusion can produce profound changes in a recipient's brain chemistry. Cases do exist where a single session of ECT results in some *shockingly* happy customers, says Dr. Gary Peebles, the director of the National Sleep Bank (and where is the humor transfusion of authentically funny jokes for Dr. Peebles? I wonder). In these cases, the administration of a strong electric current through the suffering patient's brain reverses all symptoms of catatonia and depression, breaks cycles of mania, and relieves many other plaguing shadows and diagnosable sorrows that can be found in the *DSM-XII*. Our researchers, says Dr. Peebles, are working to discover just why the delivery of sleep to a dreamless body can and does produce a full recovery for certain patients—and only a temporary reprieve for others.

To date, every former insomniac who regained the ability to sleep, post-transfusion, remains fully rehabilitated. We have no recorded relapses. No longer are these patients dependent on the sleep of strangers. Post-transfusion, they can achieve REM in their home bedrooms: Colors of their own freakish and individual manufacture flood their minds again, plots spiral up, imaginary faces and animals bubble and flume. They dream. It's heartbreaking, of course, when this does not happen. Some people, we now fear, might require weekly sleep transfusions for the rest of their lives. A blank check to float their nights.

The Slumber Corps pledges to get sleep to every insomniac "for as long as her or his need persists." That's our mission statement. Where is all that sleep going to come from, you're wondering? Us, too. Fiscally, it's a bankrupting promise. Mathematically, I'm told, it's a future lie. In five years, the Slumber Corps' monumental commitment to these insomniacs may well be an abandoned ideal, like a temple buried in the jungle. Smart people on the Slumber Corps' advisory board call our pledge a "pipe dream," as dangerous as anything we test for at the Elmhurst, New Jersey, sleep-processing plant. Yet we continue to make this promise to our incurables.

On nights when sleep continues to elude me, I consult my "zeros." My own recruitment stats.

And when even this does not work?

On my worst nights, when my eyes are burning and dawn is two hours away, I'll give up on fact, give in to fantasy. I'll shut

my eyes and pretend that Dori is receiving one of these transfusions. They were not available, of course, when she needed
them—when she lived. Which was not so long ago, not at all.
The sun rises, and she's home. Birdsong is twittering in the air,
proof of invisible birds. Dori is back in the world. Her eyes are
open on her pillow, and they are sea green and absolutely clear.
Void of all nightmares. No earthworm nest disturbs her now,
no crumb of boneyard dirt. Her waking is an instantaneous
rebirth. Her hair spools onto the pillowcase, happy memories
are coiling in her head, and tomorrow is laid out at her feet,
a net of yellow light and blue shadow that stretches from bed
frame to door.

And then?

Written out like this, you know, it sounds a little *Franken-
stein.*

Pinkly flushed, arisen, my sister startles from the room.
Grape bunches of curls spill down the back of her pajamas. She
is the age she would be today: twenty-nine.

BABY A

Last July, the Supreme Court ruled that babies could be donors, with their parents' consent. Babies are deep, rich wells for us. They serenely churn forth a pure, bracing sleep, with zero adult terror corrupting it. Since the new law went into effect, we Corps volunteers have been trying, with renewed zeal, to sign up whole families. We'll tap the parents' sleep, which is often useless to us (a fact we don't advertise, of course), just to get a baby's donation. "Pump me first," the mothers implore, so overwrought that they vitiate their draws with cortisone. We do not discuss this with the women—their polluted sleep, the futility of their generosity. We draw from parents because the experience reassures them. Really, what the nurses are draining is these mothers' fear of the unknown. They wake up, refreshed, with no memory of the draw, awash in goodwill.

Then we enroll their children in our donor program.

Four months ago, I pitched Mrs. Harkonnen at a drive outside the Piggly Wiggly grocery. I spotted a baby's face pinking out of her pretty woven papoose, and I introduced myself. Mrs. Harkonnen was an easy convert to the Slumber Corps, crying freely at Dori's death story; the baby witnessed our exchange with that eerie calm babies have, dry-eyed and blank. Was her husband with her? No? Could I arrange to speak with him, get his signature? To dispatch a Sleep Van, we'd need both parents' consent.

One week later, I paid a visit to 3300 Cedar Ridge Parkway to collect the consent forms. Mrs. Harkonnen greeted me on the porch with a shy smile, her hands starfished out in front of her; the nail polish was still wet. She'd remembered my name: "Trish! Come on in." She'd put on red lipstick, was ready with a pot of decaf. Upstairs, the baby was crying; we'd both smiled automatically at the sound. "My husband's with her. He signed your papers." She pushed over the consent form; I saw that Felix Harkonnen's autograph was freshly inked. "He's a little wor-ried about the procedure—she's our first child, you know. He's a very protective father."

The note of apology in her voice unnerved me a little; this was perhaps my first intimation that Mrs. Harkonnen was a very special sort of donor. I'd never met a mother like this, for whom the gift of a daughter's sleep seemed so matter-of-fact. Why did she assume her husband's reluctance needed explana-tion?

"But I told Felix all about those poor people on the waiting list. Why this sleep donation is so important to them. How did you call it? A 'life serum.'" Then she'd paused, staring intently at me, and I saw that I'd been wrong to think this woman was in any way naive. There was some shrewdness alive inside her kindness, a perspicacity that thrilled and frightened me, that I did not understand. The quality of Mrs. Harkonnen's attentiveness caused my whole body to prickle, as if invisible quills were lifting under my skin. This was a surprise. For the past eight months, I'd felt brain-dead and nerve-dead when I was not recruiting. I'd stumbled around in a daze during the periods between our Sleep Drives, those jagged white intervals of time, that I had formerly experienced, in unity, as "a day."

"Your sister. I can't stop thinking about her."

"Oh?"

I'd stared up at the unshaded bulb above the Harkonnens' kitchen table. Gravity can be exploited in these situations; moisture slid into my pupils. A swimmy seepage of green light contracted back inside the white bulb. I did not cry. Once the kitchen went matte again, I was able to meet her eyes:

"Well, thank you, thank you very much for keeping her in mind. My sister would be here today, if we'd had Gould's technology . . ."

Then my voice broke, and I had to really work to keep my grin from stretching into something crooked and hungry; my eyes felt suddenly dish-size, much too large for my face. Ordinarily I only resurrect Dori during a pitch. That's where I feel her. But that night I was certain that I sensed my sister's presence in that stranger's kitchen. Or almost certain. I badly wanted to see you, Dori, as you existed for Mrs. Harkonnen. Typically, my recruits receive the story of my sister's death day with a mixture of sympathy and horror; many people give sleep as a kind of frightened oblation, a way to sandbag their healthy lives from her fate; if she "works" on them, they respond with a donation. But all most people ever really know about my sister's life is how she died.

My smile became natural in response to Mrs. Harkonnen's smile as she offered me a reheat on the black coffee, cream and sugar—Mrs. Harkonnen was the kindest and gentlest inquisitor I'd ever met. Somehow she intuited all that I could not say about my sister, and she asked me only questions to which I possessed factual answers; I heard myself telling stories from our Pennsylvania childhood, these shadowy green memories of Dori that I'd never shared with any donor.

All this time, the baby had been wailing. At first, I'd been astonished by her volume. Once Mrs. Harkonnen got me talking about Dori, however, I'd stopped noticing, until I was barely aware that I was shouting to be heard. Then that pour of solar sound cut out. The infant's silence was as loud as her screams had been, at least. We turned from the forms together, and there was Mr. Harkonnen. He was standing at the top of the stairwell, holding the baby.

"I've changed my mind," he said.

I stood, and so did Mrs. Harkonnen.

"Sit down," Mrs. Harkonnen commanded me, suddenly steely. "Felix, we made a promise to these people—"

Then I went perfectly still in their kitchen, holding chilly coffee, forgotten completely—recruiting people to a cause, I've found, often isolates you in strange spandrels, caught between a stranger's intersecting planes of aversion and desire; in the case of the Harkonnens, I was a literal trespasser. "Wait here," said the red-eyed Mrs. Harkonnen, smiling sheepishly at me, as if she needed only to check on something burning in the oven. I eavesdropped on Mrs. Harkonnen's woodpecker-drilling into the stout oak of Mr. Harkonnen: "We're doing this. We have no choice. How can we live with ourselves otherwise? I won't be able to live with myself." As they argued on the stairwell, I closed my eyes and folded my hands on the kitchen table. I pictured a great fire fanning out through this house, consuming all obstacles. It was more a wish than a picture, to be honest. I'd willed the fire to eat a pathway to a yes.

I left 3300 Cedar Parkway with two signatures.

Four nights later, I dispatched a Sleep Van to the Harkonnen residence.

OUR UNIVERSAL DONOR

Baby A, on the night of that first, successful draw, was six and a quarter months old.

None of us had any clue, at that juncture, what the techs were about to uncover.

We shipped Baby A's sleep to Elmhurst, New Jersey, one of our ten processing centers. Lab technicians were amazed. Multiple tests confirmed that her sleep had zero impurities: There were no nightmare-markers, no native dream-antibodies. No need, whatsoever, for the sleep of Baby A to be sieved and purified and reconstituted.

Baby A, it turns out, is a universal donor. Nobody rejects a transfusion of her sleep.

Her discovery has been called "a boon for all humanity" by Dr. Gary Peebles. She is our dream gold mine. Banks across the country are on appeal for her sample. Lab techs work frantically to synthesize it. "Artificial sleep" has been a goal of medical researchers since the sleep banks first started operations.

Tonight will mark our sixteenth draw from Baby A. Sixteen draws in four months!

That's nearly half of Baby A's life.

December, we drew twelve hours from the baby.

In January, we bumped up to thirty-six.

In February, we started drawing the max catch for her weight.

This March, the Sleep Van has been parked on the Harkonnens' block every week.

When the numbers of insomniacs on our waiting rolls peaked, we were able to blend and redistribute the sleep of Baby A into forty-eight bodies. It was national news: "Baby A Saves the Night."

Currently Baby A is underwriting many hundreds of lives with her sleep donations, with no end to the crisis in sight. Who could have guessed that an eighteen-pound infant would have that kind of power? Who can blame Baby A's father, for abhorring our discovery?

. . .

When I pull up at 3300 Cedar Ridge Parkway, it's a little after midnight. A trio of nurses are seated in the back of the van. Outside the night is scintillating, calm. A basketball hoop in the Harkonnens' driveway keeps its monocular eye fixed on their two-toned jalopy, a brown sedan with faded turquoise doors. Large white flowers blossom all over the property in unlikely, untended spots; one clump fronds out about a foot from the Chevy's rear tires. I tell the head nurse that I want to go in alone; I perform better alone. "Are you sure, Trish?" she asks, with undisguised relief.

My regret is nearly instantaneous.

Mr. Harkonnen is standing on the lawn.

His arms are folded over his barrel chest, and the darkness lengthens and funnels around him. For a cold moment, I mistake these creased shadows for a shotgun.

"Mr. Harkonnen!" I wave, throwing my hands up, crossing the uncut grass toward him. "We've met. It's Trish Edgewater—"

"No way."

"The Corps Recruitment Manager—"

"Not tonight. We're done here."

Moonlight crosses his skin like moisture, light weeping down his craggy cheeks. He stands under the shadows of a giant poplar. Every time the boughs move in the wind, chunks of him go missing.

"Tonight, we have a true crisis on our hands, sir—"

"Is that so? Guess what I've got on my hands?"

His fists knot to form an imaginary cradle, which he swings furiously on the air.

"I've got a daughter. She needs her sleep. You show up here every goddamn week. Why can't you find someone else's kid to drain?"

Etiquette is a powerful programming, however, and easily exploitable. I sneeze. He sneezes back language at me, reflexive generosity: "Bless you." A space opens up; I inch closer on the grass: "Mr. Harkonnen, can I trouble you for five minutes of your evening? I'm asking on behalf of my dead sister, Dori Edgewater . . ." He frowns, and I score an extra second—a short tarmac—but long enough for me to launch my pitch.

Quick as I've ever managed it, I transition into Dori-mode.

Up I float; somewhere, far below me, I see a blur that is my body, pitching my sister.

"Oh, my God," he whispers when I've finished. "*That's* how she died?"

I glance down at my watch: four minutes have elapsed. A new record. "And you're saying if she'd had *one extra hour* of sleep—"

"So the coroner tells me."

The stars above the Harkonnens' brick roof are spinning. Chowdery bile rises in the back of my throat, and I stare at Mr. Harkonnen's shoes on the grass until it sinks again. I am truly spent, sweaty.

"Jesus."

Mr. Harkonnen takes a step forward with his arm lifted, as if in greeting; it falls heavily on my shoulder.

"Well, I am very sorry to hear that. Very, very sorry indeed." He whistles.

Now things get considerably more complex; at the top of the lawn, the front door to the house swings wide. The darkness spits out Mrs. Harkonnen, who joins us.

"Hel-lo!" I call out, and wince with her at the volume of my voice, which sounds deranged at this late hour with unseasonable cheer; I wonder whether the nurses can hear any of this from the van.

"I'm sorry, Justine," I blurt out. "But it's bad."

I count off the numbers in the ER.

I reveal how very little sleep we need to stave off tragedy tonight. Really, a minuscule amount from a being this tiny. We will manufacture a poly-sleep blend from it, and it will benefit hundreds of dreamless sufferers.

"The baby is inside. Felix will get her."

Head down like a linebacker, he shoulders past me on the grass, clipping me with his bicep. I gasp, surprised to enjoy the contact, even the fury behind it. It's not unlike flirtation, a move that blatant, deliberate.

"Thank you," I say, addressing the wife.

"You're welcome," grunts the husband, parking himself on the lawn again, like he can't bear to let her have the last word.

For a long moment we stand in this frozen geometry, just beyond the orange headlights of the Sleep Van. As dizzy as the stars, as close and alone. Then Mr. Harkonnen shifts his weight so that we form a true circle, and a strange joy sparks and catches in my chest.

. . .

I deliver the good news to the Sleep Van. Everybody grins with relief. Now the Sleep Van is once again an authorized vehicle on Cedar Ridge Parkway, instead of a boxy white shark waiting in the shallows to feast upon a baby. Nurse Carla swings the van into their driveway. Two nurses begin to swab the helmet with the blue solution; a third calls Jim, beaming. I decide to take a walk around the Harkonnens' neighborhood; the van is crowded, I tend to get underfoot, and I find that I do not want to be inside when Mrs. Harkonnen enters with the baby.

The Slumber Corps' lifesaving operations run on the public's trust and goodwill. Where money is concerned, we have to be careful. According to my bosses, we are working on establishing a scholarship fund for Baby A. Some kind of trust in her name. Legally, we are "just desperate," swears Jim Storch, to finagle a way to express our organization's gratitude to the family for the gift of Baby A's sleep. But this expression of gratitude must be made with diplomacy, sensitivity.

"It's delicate," Rudy tells me.

"And *muy ilegal*," echoes Jim.

Nobody in our Mobi-Van would suggest that the raw market would do a better or a fairer job of matching insomniacs and donors than the Slumber Corps. None of us can imagine the solution proposed by certain factions, "the sale of sleep," leading to an equitable system. Not that the Slumber Corps is a perfect matchmaker. Our cold calling can feel scattershot, and our dependence on strangers to refill the dream wells is total; the sleep banks are routinely on appeal for more units. You can't program omniscience into the hospital computers, and people die on the Corps' waiting lists every night. But our goal, at least, is articulable, stable, and very clear: to get clean, deep sleep to the insomniacs. I am proud to say that in its seven-year history, the Slumber Corps has never rejected an insomniac for financial reasons or requested any kind of payment.

When I registered the Harkonnens as donors, I had no idea that their daughter's sleep was a miracle in progress. Baby A is still the world's only known universal donor. But there have been several cases of sleep donations that can be accepted by a remarkable percentage of insomniacs. Three years ago, sleep found to be "highly transfusable" across many demographics was drawn from a ninety-two-year-old Swedish man in Laramie. Almost immediately after his donation, he slipped into a coma, and ever since, against the wishes of some family members, the Wyoming Slumber Corps has been "mining him" for sleep—a phrase favored by the media.

"Which is funny," Rudy snarls, "when you consider all the mining, drilling, and *earth rape* they are *actually* doing in Wyoming—and here we have this living saint, sustaining hundreds of people with his sleep."

The old man signed a contract, before losing consciousness, stipulating that he wanted his body to be farmed for sleep until its death. His last bequest. I admire the generosity of our Wyoming donor, and I invoke him at drives. But I've also had such vibrant nightmares where I see the orphaned animal of his body, tethered to Gould's machinery by the ponytail of blue wires. Strapped onto the cot, strapped into the helmet. The feet in socks.

Hundreds of lives have since been saved thanks to Baby A's donations. Many thousands more, who are wait-listed for a Baby A transfusion, have been given an EEG recording of Baby A's brain waves, transformed into an audio recording, as part of an experimental study. There is some evidence that even this remote contact with Baby A's sleep might reset insomniacs' body clocks. All of this is well documented by our outreach videos.

But Baby A's life would have been far better off, I'm certain, if I'd never found her.

. . .

The Harkonnens live in a "transitional" neighborhood—houses that you might call "fixer-uppers," or derelict, depending on how cheerful you are feeling. Even light seems hesitant to enter them. Last year, many of the rotting facades got repainted in gumball shades of pink and lime, some misguided civic project to brighten this part of our city. It's a pretty superficial shellacking—the cars and motorcycles outside are still junkers. Lawns are covered with many octaves of weeds, shading from crud brown to yellowy beige, and even the leafy trees seem to me to have too many limbs, mutating away from the rooftops in a silent, wild freedom. Several bikes knock around on their chains, an eerily genial sound, as if the machines are gossiping. Early spring, and this whole block smells like flowers. The heaving blossoms turn out to be everywhere once you notice them, overflowing the rain gutters and the sills of second-story windows, unencouraged, unsupported, and nevertheless here once more, vivid white in the night air. Beauty staging its coup in every suburb and slum in the galaxy. *You are lucky to be alive to see it, aren't you, Edgewater?* I have several canned lectures, designed to reduce my nausea after talking about Dori, which I mentally self-administer in Rudy's stern voice.

Tonight, I'm snuffed. Dori's story, now in its told state, expulsed, floats somewhere far outside me, emitting its jellyfish light. Sometimes her absence takes me over and then I'm a sleepwalker. Now, for example, as I double back to the Harkonnens.

Here they come again, the white flowers, bystanders rooted in the bright light flowing from the Sleep Van. Bodies move with their own sly life behind the windows, bending and straightening. For no easily discernible reason, I am terrified to reenter the Sleep Van. At some sore point on my revolution around the Harkonnens' block, I seem to have removed my name badge, my Corps Recruiter jacket. I'd much prefer to remain a stranger out here underneath these fragrant narcotics, the ruffling white blossoms.

I can hear the baby crying. Up ahead I see the Harkonnens' two-toned Chevy again, brown and turquoise, the basketball hoop with its frayed net. Underneath it, the Sleep Van is parked with its rear doors wide open, spilling yellow light across the lawn. Framed in the window, I see Baby A strapped to the catch-crib, her feet tensing and relaxing like little fists.

. . .

"No, no, see the bag inflating? She's still breathing on her own—"

"Get a seal on that, Carmen. Get a tighter seal on that."

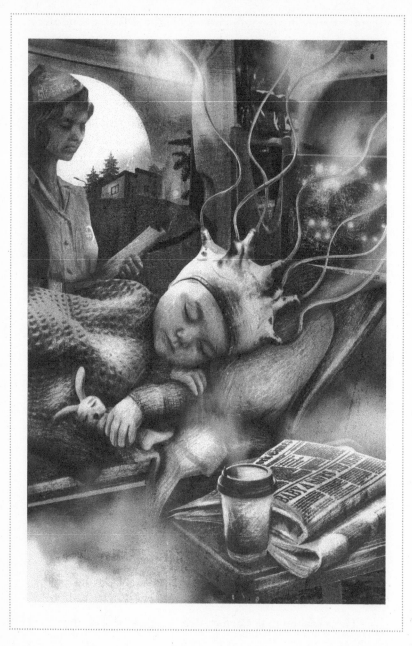

. . .

After the Harkonnen draw, we drive to the other side of town, to get a draw from Roberta Frias. Roberta is six and such a funny kid, chatty until the very second before the anesthetic crests and rolls her under. She's no Baby A. But her sleep is very useful to us, transfusable into a high percentage of insomniacs. EEGs of her first draw dazzled the nurses. Beautiful NREM— slow-wave, delta sleep, the state in which a body repairs tissue, builds bone and muscle, strengthens its immune system.

On the catch-cot, under the clear mask, her smile flutters and disappears. Her mother always dresses Roberta up for a donation, and the nurses have given up on telling her that this is unnecessary; tonight, she's wearing a frilly yellow dress covered in tiny gray mice and a pink hairband. Her parents are watching from the corner of the Sleep Van, nervous and proud. Mr. Frias, a chubby Puerto Rican pastor, taxi driver, and devoted father, a lip-biter, gives me the thumbs-up when our eyes meet.

I don't know how to describe the unique claustrophobia of a sleep-draw, if you've never been present for one, except to compare it to the electric, heavy feeling of air carrying seawater. A frightening, exhilarating charge permeates the entire atmosphere of the Sleep Van; an overpowering sense of ambient destiny, fate crushing in on all sides. This is accompanied by a nostril-flaring, neck-prickling vertigo. What provokes this disorientation, says Dr. Peebles, is your body's awareness of its proximity to an enveloping illusion—a dream, not your own, pumping out of a donor's prone form. The unhosted ghosts of these dreams in transit, en route to facilities where they will be tested, processed, and plated on ice, awaiting transfusion. World blueprints. Roberta, according to our monitors, is discharging a shocking quantity of dreams. They go soaking out of her mouth and snaking through the breathing tubes, a galaxy per millisecond. The nurses claim not to notice the smell anymore, a clay odor you can almost taste, which reminds me of the white frogs we used to net from midnight ponds, the scooped and dripping lilies.

Minutes four through eight, as the coils begin to heat: The child's fantasy is in the room with us, unexpressed in any consciousness. Her dreams glug out of her. At the end of the draw, the machinery makes a fantastic chortle, a sort of mechanical *blech*, and one nurse, Luisa, who is very uncomfortable with child donation, giggles hysterically and says, "Pardon me!"

DONOR Y

....

Two days after my last callout to the Harkonnens, Rudy Storch and I are alone in the trailer, coding for dispatch. At 9:04 p.m., the Slumber Corps' alert icon flashes onto our computer screens. Seconds later, Rudy is on the phone with Washington. They want every Corps employee present for a live broadcast, an "orientation" to some new crisis, set to air in an hour's time.

They're calling it the worst scandal in the sleep bank's seven-year history.

"Oh, fuck me," says Rudy, glued to the screen. "Get everybody in."

. . .

Here is what we learn in the hours that follow:

On March 23, a man whom the media is calling "Donor Y" walked into a sleep bank in San Diego and asked to register. It was his first time donating sleep. According to his file, he is a forty-two-year-old white male, five feet seven, 189 pounds, 128/67 blood pressure, no sexual partners sharing the bed with him, no children. He checked no on all the disqualifying boxes:

Sleep apnea: no. Sleepwalking: no. He was next handed the CDC alphabetized list of all three hundred known contagious nightmares—

- ☐ Abomination, horned
- ☐ Ambulance, frozen yellow siren
- ☐ Anthill, no queen
- ☐ Ants, flesh-eating
- ☐ Aorta, burst
- ☐ Asteroid, green
- ☐ Attic, grandmother's ghost
- ☐ Attic, padlocked toy chest
- ☐ Avalanche, death of self
- ☐ Avalanche, death of spouse
- ☐ Avalanche, live burial

Et cetera. Donor Y did not check a single box.

For the past seven years, the CDC has been working in collaboration with every local branch of the Slumber Corps to keep a Dream Database. The CDC monitors the occurrence of communicable nightmares in order to detect trends and to track and investigate outbreaks of similar dreams in certain regions, "nightmare clusters." Odds ratios, based on logistic regression models, are used to calculate the risk of infection from exposure to a sick dreamer.

Donor Y self-reported clean. "Baby-like, fetal position" was what he wrote on his questionnaire in response to "Describe your sleep posture." His handwriting is neat and evenly spaced; the only unusual thing about it is that Donor Y wrote in tiny all capitals, like a scream shrunken into a whisper. Having passed the health prescreen, he donated a twelve-hour unit of sleep—

the legal limit for a man his age and weight. Nothing occurred during the draw to put the nurses on alert.

His sleep was transported to the Berkeley testing and processing center; two days later, it was shipped to sleep banks all over the country. The nightmare may have been undetectable by standard testing. It may have been perfectly detectable and somehow missed by the technicians. What is known: Donor Y's sleep was flagged as "healthy," centrifugally spun, and packaged into "Sleep Blend G-17," an amalgam of hundreds of donations designed to neutralize and dilute any residual impurities from single donors. Sleep blends are prepared for rapid delivery to the widest spectrum of insomniacs.

Early estimates suggested that anywhere from one thousand to ten thousand patients might have been infected with Donor Y's nightmare. Within hours of the alert, lawsuits are being threatened—the Slumber Corps is charged with failing to adequately screen volunteer donors and test their sleep.

"Donors are given a questionnaire about their history of sleep disturbance," says a spokeswoman for the Slumber Corps, Betsy Gamberri. They dressed her in dizzy-tall stilettos and a pink bolero with linebacker shoulder pads, as if seeking to increase her literal stature in the medical community.

"The onus is on donors. You have to self-report your nightmares. The questionnaire, if answered correctly, should have eliminated him."

"Either the donor did not know he was infected with this nightmare or he lied," says Dr. Peebles.

Currently, the identity of Donor Y is being kept secret from the public—if it is, in fact, known. This omission stretches to accommodate the wildest theories: rumors of sabotaged files, internal Slumber Corps conspiracies.

"Have you ever *been* to the San Diego bank, Trish?" whispers my colleague Jeremy in the Mobi-Van. "If the guy's file went missing, I'm sure it was just some administrative fuck-up."

Jeremy does our branch's data entry, and I guess he knows whereof he speaks. We agree that it's far scarier, in its way, to think that a teenage volunteer with bangs in his eyes, some good-hearted college kid named Brad or Boomer, simply forgot to scan a state ID. You can see why the theorists are getting so much airtime. There's something darkly reassuring about imagining a cabal under the earth, or a government plot, or any human scheme, to undergird the spread of his "plague dream."

What follows is a catastrophe for the Corps beyond our own worst institutional nightmares.

The Donor Y scandal causes a nationwide drought in all the sleep banks.

People are scared to donate. Many decide that Gould's procedure must be hazardous. Their fear adheres to the physical apparatus: the silver helmet, the mask, and the catch-cot. Myths run rampant, a parallel contagion: *What if you can contract a nightmare in the Sleep Vans? What if donors, too, expose themselves to the infection?* Other donors dread *becoming* a Donor Y. Newscasters transmit the germ of fear to millions. The morning news, the evening news, it's relentless:

"Obviously, the American people have been lied to. The American people have been misled about *the real risks* of this sleep donation procedure."

Never have I heard "the American people" invoked so many times per hour.

The CDC assembles a task force of dream epidemiologists.

In the Mobi-Van, we are calling around the clock, reassuring old donors, begging. The intern jokes that he could use some bootleg sleep himself, until Rudy roars at him to knock it off.

If you've ever watched people speedily disqualify themselves from serving on a jury in a courtroom, you can imagine the efficiency with which many of our cold calls recuse themselves. When I announce that I am a Slumber Corps recruiter, people launch into descriptions of their most bewildering dreams, as evidence that they are unfit to give:

"Ma'am, I keep drowning in my own blood at night. I have the shadow of an insect, I dreamed that. Really, I'm a menace. My dreams aren't right."

"This one I've been having since childhood. I call it the bottomless dream? The dead go spelunking into blue holes. Then for some reason I'm in Lithuania, in a jade cave where the tornadoes breed."

"President Nixon strapped to a fire truck! Twice, I dreamed that this month."

A recent widower says: "What lugubrious facts. I regret that I will be unable to change them for you. My wife just died, you see, and she's saturated my sleep like coffin milk."

A Russian woman interrupts my scripted pitch to scream at me, quite persuasively: "I should ask *you*; you should give *me*. Every hour I have, I need!"

It's a crisis of faith. Donors refuse to give sleep; donees who have spent months on our rolls are now refusing the transfusions. Suddenly, impossibly, we must advertise to recruit the sick ones.

We need good sleepers and we need insomniacs. To combat attrition on two fronts, the Slumber Corps launches a new PR campaign. The TV spots show scrupulously groomed young couples, paragons of hygiene, holding up their children under a pristine full moon, yawning, smiling, waiting for their turn to donate at a Suburban Donation Station. Behind the van is a tract house and snail-shaped driveway. The message: the Sleep Van comes to you. Then the camera cuts to footage of a yellow nursery. There is zoo wallpaper, the zany chandelier of a baby mobile. The camera floats over a crib, pans down to a three-month-old infant's seamless eyelid. A lavender bib with tiny sheep rises and falls on her perfect chest, with a dreamy evenness.

SLEEP LIKE A BABY AGAIN:
1-800-IMAWAKE

It's like watching food advertising for hungry mouths.

We run a local hotline. On either side of me, Yoon and Jeremy are pouring reassurances into their telephone headsets. These salving phrases are the antibodies engineered for us by the Corps scientists, sets of facts to counteract the spread of doubt, terror. And as we speak them, we try hard to immunize ourselves, and one another, against the panic of the callers. "The Donor Y contagion is officially contained," I say on repeat a hundred times a night. When I close my eyes, though, I picture a microscopic worm nuzzling under skin, blood-rocketed through the entire organ system.

"The needy simply do not trust us," complains Rudy Storch.

"I can't believe this," says Jim, shaking his head.

Very slowly, Jim reads off the names of Last Day insomniacs who have requested removal from our transfusion waiting list: "Rita dropped out? Melissa Van Ness? Has everybody lost their mind?"

Reflexively, he keeps thumbing water from his eyes. Rudy

has formulated a sort of chitinous shell of sarcasm to protect himself, but I worry about Jim.

"Jesus. I mean, mistrust us, okay, think us diabolical, but let us help you."

I don't tell Jim or Rudy that certain people on their staff mistrust *them*; that we all wonder at the brothers' motivations for pouring their fortune into the Corps.

Chief among the skeptics is Roger Kleier, the Slumber Corps janitor. He is always recruiting our doughy new interns to share his suspicions of the Storches. He is on the payroll; he is not a volunteer. His salary comes from the tremendous endowment made to our regional branch by Jim and Rudy Storch. Every month, an influx from the brothers' coffers fills his bank account.

"You gotta be shitting me! The toilet brothers give up a million-dollar business to work out of a trailer—*why*?"

Roger is a naturally suspicious person. There are bodies that reject sleep transfusion after sleep transfusion. Bodies that come preprogrammed with evolved defenses against all foreign dreams, that respond to even infant sleep transfusions with a violent immune reaction. And goodness knows, I have worked with many people in this waking life who seem congenitally incapable of accepting any human donation of blood, marrow, sleep, criticism, praise, money, or love. Some days, I know, I'm one of them. You find that you're not a match with the donor. Or you sense that the gift will take some freedom from you. Your body rebels, maybe you don't even know why. But the donation is rejected.

Roger's janitorial desire to get a clean read on the Storches, his hostile curiosity about their motives, adds its resonance to the chorus that pours through my headset. During Phone

Shifts, I read my updated script. I say: "The Donor Y out-break was an anomaly." I say: "Sleep donation is safer at this moment than it has ever been in history." I say what I can say, and mean: "People are lying awake, dying. They need your help."

On a good night, I feel I've done a good thing. That donors will continue to replenish the sleep banks; that the risks to them are minimal; that the benefits to the insomniacs are incalculable, sky-wide, as enormous as any life-in-progress.

On a bad night, this can feel like stitching an imaginary net under a hundred wheeling acrobats. Or promising the stars they'll never burn out, fall. The Corps script doesn't come with stage directions; I could ease up a little on the operatic vibrato of my promises. Politicians would retire their office before guaranteeing so many splendid tomorrows to their voters. Men don't lie like this to get women into bed.

Underneath my audible solicitations, I make another request, at a frequency far below the chittering of my transmissions to these people, my bullshit reassurances: *Please let what I'm telling them stay true, please let them be safe?*

. . .

Donor Y.

Why, why.

I become obsessed with him.

Was it a case of "malice aforethought"?

This term I learned from a high school book, *Moby-Dick*: a white whale ramming with blind hate into the hull of a boat, trying to kill everyone aboard.

"Malice aforethought," the teacher explained, meant the whale could scheme, like a human, and design its revenge.

Perhaps Donor Y wanted to settle some score with the universe. Perhaps Donor Y was tired of being an anonymous sufferer in a crowd and wanted to propagate his worst night. Gould's machines gave him a way to tattoo his private horror onto the minds of strangers. This possibility—an uncomfortably arousing possibility—gets mentioned in every news story about the crisis. Villains sell papers. And I find that I prefer him this way: nasty, aware.

Donor Y, when I try to picture him, never develops a face. What I see instead is a husk, a humanoid virus, interested only in the dissemination and replication of its own pain.

You've heard about that sperm donor whose single cup of swimmers went on to sire legions of snub-nosed, blond half brothers and sisters? Our Donor Y has inseminated thousands of dreamers with his personal hell. He's broadcast his nightmare to every demographic.

Donor Y, Baby A. I picture them as opposite poles on an axis. Donor Y, pumping out the nightmare, and Baby A, pumping out black sleep.

I find that I badly want Donor Y to be pure as well: purely evil.

And if he betrays me by showing up, becoming real? Just some middle-aged guy in a sweater, with one uncommonly virulent nightmare? This scenario, I hate: Donor Y gave no thought at all to the possibility that he might be such a carrier. He was a sincere do-gooder. He saw a flyer and wandered up to a registrant. An earnest brunette administrator ran down the questionnaire with him in the lunar-lit tent, and both of them believed that his responses were honest.

Last April, Rudy and Jim had me tell "Dori's Story" at the Corps Sweet Dreams Benefit—our largest annual fundraiser. At the ball, I stuttered, lost my place twice. I torpedo-sneezed into an audience of billionaires.

"No, Edgewater!" Rudy reassured me. "You got half the room with that. That snot was a good touch! I mean, I know it wasn't a 'touch'—with you, it's never a performance—"

In the bathroom, I rinsed my eyes. A German woman approached me, a Deutsche Bank widow in shimmering green. She complimented me, in her way, on the purity of my grief: "Still so sad! After all these years and tellings!"

I've shared Dori with thousands of people now: reporters and talk show hosts; reluctant sleep donors; once, a jet-lagged, baffled, yet receptive Spanish prince at a strange and endless state lunch. Every single time I tell it, I go into convulsions. I show her photograph.

"She's like a grief hemophiliac," Rudy told the German widow, who was searching avidly for her checkbook; for an instant, we locked eyes over the sequined shoulder pad of this woman's evening gown. "It doesn't clot. It never runs dry."

Is our appeal to this alpha breed of ego a bad thing? Rudy argues that it's one of our greatest accomplishments—that the Corps reorients the flow of ego, like the old river-dammers who got the water to run backward and irrigate a dry world. We at the Slumber Corps are hydraulic engineers. We redistribute funds, dreams, to eradicate thirst. And I don't disagree; only it's a strange way to help the living, to continually dredge her up, my sister.

I've been giving a lot of thought to the similarities between what I do and what's been done by Donor Y. Thanks to my efforts, millions of people are infected with Dori's last breath. My job, as I understand it, is to compel our donors to feel the horror of her death. To "spread awareness."

"It won't bring her back," a trustee once told me soapily over another endless Slumber Corps charity spaghetti dinner, as if lathering his own hands with this antiseptic wisdom. Which, oh God, caused me to swallow a small withered tomato whole so I could hiss across the table, "I *know* that!"

At the same time, what am I doing, if not reseeding my dead sister into as many fertile minds and bodies as possible?

DORI

....

Sometimes I think the right doctor could open my chest and find her there, my sister, frozen inside me, like a face in a locket.

DONOR Y AND THE
ELECTIVE INSOMNIACS

Ten days after Donor Y's story breaks, the San Francisco ER admits a group of twenty chattering maniacs who are refusing sleep. Every one of them tests positive for the Donor Y nightmare. These people were not our patients. They did not receive transfusions from American sleep banks. They were passengers on Flight 109, from Havana to SFO. Immediately, the passengers become misery-celebrities. They represent an entirely new species of revenant in our midnight world.

We learn that these people were part of a group of sixty-one medical tourists. As recently as a week ago, not one of these twenty new victims of the nightmare contagion could fall asleep. Either unwilling or unable to wait another night on the Slumber Corps rolls, they'd chartered a flight to Cuba and paid to receive an experimental sleep transfusion. They spent a week recovering in Havana, cocooned in a secret room behind the Hospital Hermanos Ameijeiras, near the leafy gold light and the shining *bahía*. Sleeping and dreaming, assimilating the transfusion.

During that time, the Cuban doctors confirmed that twenty of the twenty-two American recipients had regained their ability to fall asleep on their own. As happens in the best-case scenarios, a single transfusion had jolted them into their original sleep/wake cycles. The return flight to San Francisco should have been a beautiful milestone for these people: stars shuttling past the cabin windows, the recovered insomniacs drifting into natural sleep. Half an hour into the flight, the steward reported hearing piercing screams throughout the cabin. A fifty-three-year-old male passenger from North Carolina, snoring in a middle seat, 13B, was the first to present symptoms of the Donor Y nightmare. Soon half a dozen other passengers seemed to be plummeting into the same dream, and then the howls came at regular intervals, according to the steward at the press conference, "everyone screaming at once, the way a Ferris wheel sounds, like they were all going in circles."

The Corps was not unaware that such medical tourism occurred. They had reports of sleep transfusions being offered for cash already underway in Cuba, Vietnam, Haiti, western Germany, despite headquarters' issued warnings to American insomniacs regarding these "back-alley dream dealers," decrying their lack of oversight and regulation, their profit hunger, their shabby facsimiles of Gould's machines. What nobody knows is how the Cubans wound up with units of the tainted sleep in the first place.

Fusillades of educated speculation erupt on our TVs:

1. Units of the infected sleep have crossed the ocean, through some black-market transaction.
2. An American who received one of the tainted sleep transfusions gave—or sold—her infected sleep abroad.

And then things shade into hysteria, with some people alleging that the Donor Y pathogen has gone airborne. What if it was sneezed out, coughed up, a scum of germs on skin? What if it was transmitted to all the passengers via the recycled air of the plane?

The Corps issues a press release: NIGHTMARE-PRIONS CAN *ONLY* BE TRANSMITTED THROUGH SLEEP TRANSFUSIONS. The Donor Y nightmare cannot be contracted orally, or through skin. It is not an airborne virus. It is not transmitted through insect bites, food, water, or sexual contact with a sick dreamer. There is no risk of transmission to a sleep donor.

But this does not halt the proliferation of paranoiac theories regarding motive, transmission.

It feels like a moment in history. Even in the present, you get that shivery sense, watching the greenish footage of Flight 109 parked on the tarmac, the circular door to this winged hospice opening and releasing the victims of the outbreak down spindly stairs. "You look like you've seen a ghost"—an expression I've known since childhood, and never once had the occasion to use. These descending people on the TV screen look like they've seen worse. Several older men are crying, their shoulders hiccuping up and down under the red Slumber Corps blankets. In the hospital, they won't pull their heads through the teal pajama holes. They don't dare blink. They pry their lids open with thumb and forefinger; some beg for stitches, tape.

The doctors are calling them "elective insomniacs."

The doctors have begun to forcibly sedate some of these patients, at their request, since they are incapable of mastering their terror of sleep.

The goal of the electives: to stay conscious. To never again cycle into REM.

And then we learn that the passengers of Flight 109 are not the only ones, that hundreds of other victims of the Donor Y contagion are refusing to sleep.

It's startling how quickly their terror changes everything for us.

People are confused by the new taxonomy of insomnia: Wait, these twenty insomniacs make a full recovery in Cuba, they have one bad dream, and they give up on sleep *for good*? So they are infected with a nightmare. What in God's name could be so frightening that death seems preferable to sleeping? What are they seeing, at night?

Newspapers are not even printing descriptions of the Donor Y nightmare. There is great concern that readers will convert the words into a copycat dream, causing waves of hypochondria, mass hysteria. As a protection, this press embargo strikes me as unnecessary—none of the infected patients can tell us anything of substance about the Donor Y nightmare, even after experiencing it for dozens of nights in a row. As one infected woman stammers in a radio interview, the Donor Y nightmare does not translate into "upstairs language." Her speech was cold and precise, the words crisply etched against the silence, so that when I closed my eyes what I saw was not the dream but snowflakes, these soluble blue skeletons falling through space. What she could say about the dream melted quickly away, like a visitation from another world entirely.

Doctors at the sleep clinics are working with teams of psychiatrists at the VA hospitals, hoping to replicate their success at getting PTSD-afflicted veterans to "risk" a night's sleep. As far as elective insomnia goes, that's our closest precedent: war veterans who are afraid to sleep, who dread their nightly redeployment to the Mekong Delta or Kabul, and the wet red scenes that might recur in dreams while they are trapped behind their eyelids.

The horrible symmetry of the reversal is rich fodder for late-night TV comedians, jowly theologians, the news anchors with their sibilant pity, their masks of skin and hair. Ratings spike. Panic spikes. Windows shine late into the night, every home in America shingled in yellow rectangles of light, until it seems like entire neighborhoods are having allergic reactions to the Donor Y crisis; even people with no history of insomnia or dream transfusions are suddenly frightened to crawl into bed.

The National Sleep Bank establishes a hotline for concerned citizens.

Callers accuse any human volunteer who answers in a breathless singsong, like betrayed children: "You said this couldn't happen!"

If we failed, admits Dr. Peebles, it was a failure of imagination. Contagion itself: Early on, we foresaw this as a danger. We took the appropriate precautions. After early clinical trials of Gould's machine showed certain nightmare prions could be passed from body to body, every laboratory in the country joined forces. New tests were developed: sleep assays, dream immunoblots. All donated sleep in this country is subjected to a rigorous screening and purification process.

But this specific outcome of a nightmare contagion? "Elective insomnia"? This was unforeseeable. This was unpreventable. Who alive could have guessed that one San Diego man's bad dream—no matter how frightening—could make patients *nostalgic* for their insomnia?

A new mental illness, some psychiatrists are eager to label it.

A kind of extreme sleep-anorexia.

Iatrogenic: a word that sends me to the dictionary. More

deadpan comedy: it means our "lifesaving" transfusions have provoked a secondary insomnia. The cure is worse than the disease.

Some begin to speculate: *Was* this done by design? Is Donor Y a new kind of bioterrorist, who co-opted Gould's technology to stage an attack?

Some are beginning to believe he is the actual ungulate. The red-horned devil himself.

I'm so stunned that when I answer calls, my mind's a blank. I let my mouth reel off the Corps' press release: "Now, more than ever before, the world needs your gift of sleep."

Elsewhere, the elective insomniacs are taking increasingly drastic measures to escape the REM cycle. They latch their eyeballs open, *A Clockwork Orange* self-torture. Abuse amphetamines. The most desperate electives will not seek treatment in the hospital, preferring instead the slow, excruciating death of sleep refusal. "Opting out," Jim calls this.

BABY A

....

Breaking news: Several of the Flight 109 passengers receive emergency transfusions spun out of the Baby A donations, and doctors make yet another discovery. Shock-deliveries of Baby A's untainted sleep can flush such nightmares out of the system. Glad tidings for the world, at last. A van screams over to the Harkonnen residence. More panacea-sleep gets pumped out of her.

Within a twenty-four-hour span, the seven infected passengers who receive a transfusion of Baby A's sleep are cleared of the Donor Y nightmare.

The Baby A miracle is cheered by everyone, everywhere, with the powerful exception of our star donor's father. Felix Harkonnen, on receiving the news that his daughter's transfusions can eradicate Donor Y's contagious nightmare: "They need her sleep, too? All these new people? My God, can't you folks find another body to snatch here? Another of these universal donors? You're telling me my kid's the only one?" We both picture her then: somebody else's daughter, playing Wiffle ball, riding her yellow bike to school, sleeping like a champ. "Go scout new talent, why don't you?" he growled. "Scour the nursing homes. Find a hundred-year-old man. I don't want my daughter's first birthday to be in a Sleep Van."

Baby A's supply cannot meet the increased demand. Her tiny body can produce only so many hours of sleep per week. Hundreds less than we need, it turns out, at the sleep banks.

When I schedule my next visit to 3300 Cedar Ridge Parkway, I am deliberate about choosing a time when I know that Felix Harkonnen will not be home. Mrs. Harkonnen invites me in. She brings out a plate of sugar cookies and switches the television on, which permits us to crouch like spies on the orange sofa and whisper to each other, safely enclosed inside a bubble of background noise.

"Tell me about your sister," says Mrs. Harkonnen.

"You want to hear it again?"

"Can you stand to tell it again?"

"Okay."

I am certain that Mrs. Harkonnen has no desire to hear another word about Dori; she is pushing me to make some reciprocal give, I think. Asking for a trade.

"Go on——" she prods. "I'm all ears."

She leans back on the sofa, knocking the cork soles of her slippers on the glass table, her robe flapping open. I can see a swirl of mauve moles on her collarbone, the elastic band of her nursing bra biting into her pale left breast.

"This was my sister," I tell her, extracting the photograph from my bag.

Unconsciously, half-consciously, I know we are both participating in the illusion that my sister is the one they will be helping. I brandish her photograph before Mrs. Harkonnen's eyes, then my own, letting the spell set. Dori's suffering I describe so freshly that anyone could be forgiven for forgetting that it's over, forever.

"We need to live as one body, don't we, Trish?" she asks me, her blue eyes widening inches from my face.

Mrs. Harkonnen and I have never talked religion, or gotten into her family background, but I suspect that something must have shattered her in a complementary way, to make her such a perfect match for my sister's story. Maybe she, too, lost a sister. Maybe she belongs to a strict sect that advocates the gift of one's every breath to strangers.

But all my assumptions, Justine Harkonnen reverses. The physics of giving and receiving, as I understand them, seem not to apply here. Even to a van filled with Slumber Corps evangelists, her faith in the rightness of sleep donation is alarming. She gives what we demand, with blue eyes scrubbed of any misgivings. We all find this upsetting, I know it, although there's not much room to say so. Nurse Carmen speaks her name with a censuring wonder. Nurse Luisa, who has three little boys, won't make eye contact with Mrs. Harkonnen any longer. A good mother, the nurses nervously agree, should be growing *more* upset with us, *more* worried for her baby's health, *angrier* about our chronic requests—not less.

I follow the Harkonnens into the Sleep Van. Milk darkens a quarter-inch circle around Mrs. Harkonnen's left nipple, an involuntary seepage of which she seems wholly unaware; underneath the giraffe-print blanket, black sleep gushes out of her daughter.

There are natural laws that govern the flow of dream and substance from body to body, laws that determine the passage of electricity through tissue, the routes taken by ruby marrow and iodine crystals and colorless vibrations. Laws to order every visible and invisible migration.

And I feel certain there must be a second set of laws, inscrutable but real, that governs exactly how much an individual can give to and receive from another. Some hydrology of human generosity. Because there are these gifts we can make to one another freely, reflexively, with no sting of loss; and there are gifts we fight to relinquish, beg to get.

Mr. Harkonnen grabs me while the nurses adjust the baby's silver helmet. Nurse Carmen, frowning, flicks at a gummed tube.

"You have pushed beyond the limits of what she can spare," growls Mr. Harkonnen.

"We have not," I say sadly.

I show him the chart:

PATIENT'S WEIGHT: __19 lbs__

MAXIMUM IN ONE SLEEP DRAW: __6 hrs__

MAXIMUM IN A 30-DAY PERIOD: __54 hrs__

"Well, what did you take just now?"

"Six hours."

His eyes search my face.

"You're sure it's safe for her to give that much?"

Oh, I have no idea. Safety is nothing we can guarantee to a donor; that's why I collect the signatures.

"These days, the science is so advanced! Trust me, our sleep doctors know every vital detail pertaining to your daughter. They will take only what her body can afford to give, I absolutely promise you."

Midway through the draw, there is some hiccup; a green light blinks on above the monitors and we all wince, even the nurses. Which is a frightening thing to witness, this neon beeping registering on the nurses' napkin-smooth faces—something akin to watching stewardesses flinch at midflight turbulence. Then the regular rhythms resume, draining more sleep from her chest. The Sleep Van fills with the odd slick smell, and the proprietary gurgle of the machine.

In her womb, Baby A was formed inside a tidaling generosity. Glucose, oxygen, proteins, fats: all transferred from the mother's bloodstream to the bloodstream of the baby.

INTERMISSION:
FAITH TRANSFUSION

You start to feel like it's all a Ponzi scheme.

I have to go into the Storches' private office in the trailer, to let the brothers administer to me.

I want to know: Do they think I should do my pitch a different way?

Jim scowls up at me from his office chair with good-natured bemusement, as if he's trying to locate the humor in a very bad joke. Rudy speaks in a tone like knuckles cracking:

"The Donor Y furor is negatively affecting your pitching. Is that the problem?"

Yes, I say. One of them.

There is microsleep; there is also microarousal. The brain's partial awakening. At the cerebral disco, parts of the brain are always lighting up, going dark. I'm waking up, I tell the Storches. When I pitch, I am in two places at once—asleep, awake—merged with Dori, but also observing myself from above. There I am, far below, in a mall parking lot; I stagger backward as if shot. But I can also see beyond my body now, to the faces of my recruits. I can hear the threat encoded in my pitch. People go sheet-white, their heads shaking to the Dori-rhythms. Children hide behind their parents' legs, but they watch me, too, and they know that if their parents do not give sleep, if they "choose" not to donate, they, too, might die in this same juddering, blood-sputtering, irremediably conscious way.

"And the problem is, what, that you feel guilty?"

I nod.

"Don't. Problem solved."

"It's this Donor Y bullshit. She's scared, Rudy."

"What would really be a nightmare for us? If you quit pitching, at a time when we need every minute we can get of REM sleep."

Jim is pacing now, so agitated he won't look my way.

"If a takedown of our charity was something you planned, Donor Y?" says Jim, addressing the wavy blankness of a window. "Mission accomplished."

Does Jim talk to Donor Y, too? Is he the imaginary target for all of Jim's anger? This fills me with a great sorrowful surprise. We have a phantom in common. I wonder how he appears to Jim, if he is a bearded terrorist, if he is an insane person, if he is perfect evil. Whoever he turns out to be, his dream has spawned actual fatalities. Thirty-two "suicides" have been linked to the Donor Y nightmare. ("Suicides" is another term being hotly debated at this moment, since many of the Donor Y–infected appear to have scaled ladders and jumped from catwalks and rooftops in a somnambulant fugue.) He incubated all those deaths, not one life.

Then Rudy brightens, turning to me.

"Have you seen your zeros this month? With the Baby A aggregates? That will be cheering. Get those percentages for her, Jim—"

Worse, I've started to hear my doubts in Dori's voice. She was always smarter than me, in school, outside school. If she were here, I would ask her what to do now. She's not a word-talker, not anymore, but her pressure inside my rib cage translates quite clearly: *This is how you turn a gift into extortion.*

"I think I have to try to find another way of pitching . . ."

"Baby," cautions Jim, "you need to calm down, now."

"And I don't want to terrify . . ."

"Oh," says Rudy. "Edgewater."

Jim's face unpetals, revealing some trembling emotion belied by his groomed silver brows, his Storchy I'm-on-your-side smile. Rage, I think.

"Jesus, Trish," Jim murmurs. "We're already so fucked here."

Behind Jim, the trailer windows are flatly sparkling. At this hour, they are black rectangles. It's unnerving to look out, see nothing.

"I hate that I'm always scaring everyone. Bullying them into giving."

"Don't be. That's not helpful."

"That's a waste of your talents."

"Your energies, baby. They're finite."

"Take that fear and put it out there."

"Put it *in* them—"

"Get the hours, Edgewater. People are dying."

"You're one of the most valuable members of our team, Edgewater."

"Look, we want donors to feel good about the gift they are making? But let's just say, hypothetically, that they feel bad, or scared? Does that change the quality of the gift, Edgewater? No."

Doesn't it matter how you ask the question? Or if the tone of your request is closer to a fist than to an open palm? Can the nature of the request corrupt the purity of the gift, the donated sleep? How stupid. How could it. A unit of sleep is a unit of sleep, say my bosses. People have free will; they give if they want to, don't if they don't.

I nod, relieved. What they say washes over me, washes in. *Oh, let it,* I think. *Stop making everything wrong.*

"What better cause can you imagine?"

"Do the math on that."

"You're doing good work, Trish."

"Keep up the good work, Edgewater."

"Thanks, guys."

This is what I want to believe, and now, with their assistance, believe again.

FIELD TRIP

....

When the Storches return from their DC leadership retreat, they are almost unrecognizably gung ho. In our trailer, they mandate enthusiasm for the zillion Corps initiatives. "Field Trips" being one of these:

INITIATIVE 499-B, FIELD TRIPS: "In the interests of greater accountability, we want to show Slumber Corps' donors the direct impact of their sleep donations."

Proposed venues: the regional sleep banks, the sleep hospices, and our downtown hospital, where donors can visit Ward Six, Orexins, and Ward Seven, Elective Insomniacs.

"I vote Ward Seven," says Rudy. He uses that verb as a courtesy, as if we have equal say in the matter. "You chaperone, Edgewater. We want the Harkonnens to meet the electives."

"We're allowed up for that? Nonfamily?"

"It's all arranged. It's a meet and greet. You introduce Justine and Felix to the Baby A waiting list."

"That way, you know, obverse-reverse? They'll understand *exactly* what Baby A's sleep means to these people." Jim beams at me. "Show them. She's a miracle. She's the best hope for these electives."

Rudy adds, "Don't fuck it up."

"Right," I say.

Rudy lends me his Prius.

The Harkonnens are standing on their lawn when I arrive.

Nobody sits next to me.

Somehow, I got it into my head that Mrs. Harkonnen *wanted* to meet the electives. That she had a maternal curiosity about these people wait-listed for her daughter's sleep. So it's a shocker when Mrs. Harkonnen in her pretty new dress, with its flouncy hemline, the pink and blue flowers, turns from Mr. Harkonnen to me in the boss's car and says, "You might have to hold my hand, both of you."

"She's afraid," Mr. Harkonnen translates. When he's forced to talk to me now, whatever he says, it's like a hoof stirring turf: red blood floods his face. We've known each other for four months, Mr. Harkonnen and I. He has never suggested that I call him Felix.

"I'm not afraid, Felix. I just don't want to embarrass anybody."

She undoes her seat belt. I hear the click, panic.

We're still three miles from the hospital, I tell Justine.

Then she wraps her arms around my headrest, launches forward in a whisper: "Trish? I do worry that I might get a little emotional."

"Emotional?"

And in the seconds and minutes that follow, I start to realize how wedded I've become to my fantasy of this woman. To me, she is a superhuman. Freakishly calm, freakishly generous, freakishly strong, in her opaque convictions. I check the rearview for confirmation of this impression. In the back seat, Justine's face looks grainy white, her shoulders slump. Her face is terrified.

I park the Prius in the visitor lot. Ward Seven may be new, but the visitor lot looks unchanged to me. There's a Honda in my old spot, in the shade of the lone tree; years ago, I tell Justine, that's where I liked to park when I came here to see Dori.

Ward Seven opened without ceremony, no ribbon-cutting, a week after the mass infection of Flight 109. Seventy-nine people in our city received transfusions of the tainted sleep. Seventeen of them now do their sleeping here. These people have checked themselves into Ward Seven because they are terrified of falling into the dream and too frightened to sleep at home. They badly want to live; and so, with the aid of hypnotics, under the doctors' supervision, they get sent back into the hell of the REM cycle. It's an unspeakably brave act, say the sleep doctors who work with this population. To ask for that help. To accept the monstrous costs. "Do I wake up rested?" I heard a patient laugh bitterly on the radio. "Are you crazy? Every night is a rematch with his nightmare. But they tell me if I don't dream at all, I'll die." In the Mobi-Van, we have photocopies of several of the Ward Seven electives' authorization forms to show our donors. It's very moving to me, to see their signatures on the consents.

On Ward Seven, there is a glass partition.

"Look at them," Mrs. Harkonnen breathes.

The room behind the glass is so dark, it takes a moment to see what's caught Mrs. Harkonnen's eye. Short beds bracket the shadows. Orderlies walk along the aisle, misting the patients' heads like cabbage rows, attaching the electrodes that will monitor their sleep. These patients are also research subjects, who submit nightly to polysomnography, who offer up their infected sleep for study.

Staring into Ward Seven, we sway slightly, as if we are out to sea.

"My heart is really pounding," murmurs Mrs. Harkonnen. So Mr. Harkonnen and I draw around her like parentheses. We each take a hand. Justine turns her blue eyes from Felix's face to mine with an almost-animal faith; the look of a leashed creature who presumes she's being led somewhere for a reason. It's the same look, incidentally, that the patients are giving the orderlies.

This field trip, I decide, was a terrible idea. I don't like the firing-squad ratio of thin dreamers to burly male orderlies. I don't want to watch these poor people go dark or see anyone get pillow-smothered by the doctors' hypnotics. I can't stand the thought of the Donor Y dream slinking through them, awaiting its opportunity to flash into reality. Despite everything I know about the nightmare's transmission, and the "Facts, Not Fears" campaign; despite the reverb of my own voice chanting panic-antidotes into the blue Corps telephones; despite what I publicly avow to believe about the "contained" contagion, and the humble, human origins of the Donor Y nightmare prion—I am grateful for this glass. Out here, we're safe. We are moated by health.

"We're just going to watch them?" says Mr. Harkonnen. "Like the bears in the damn zoo?"

"I guess so."

I think we're all relieved to be on this side of the Ward Seven partition.

When I was a kid, and the "good sleeper" in our family, I'd lie on my back and cramp with a wretched pleasure, knowing my sister was awake, and feeling with delicate, bird-footed certainty that my own eyelids would soon flutter, and I would be off. This I labeled "the bad-bad feeling." It was my relief, and what I can now identify as the baseless smugness of the healthy. I loved my sister, but by age nine I'd learned already to hedge that love with revulsion, afraid that I would catch her problem.

"Miss Edgewater!" A taffy pull of an Indian man, six foot seven and El Greco thin, comes flapping down the hallway. "And these must be the famous sires of Baby A!" Mrs. Harkonnen giggles nervously. He introduces himself as Dr. Glasheen, a fellow at the National Sleep Bank. "Okay, thanks for waiting. Had to get you folks in the system. Here are your bracelets. We're going in."

Dr. Glasheen hits a button. The glass partition begins to retract into the wall.

Here is what it feels like, to visit Hell at Dusk. Park your boss's Prius outside this county hospital. Step into Ward Seven's Sleep Incubation Chamber: The warm dark swallows you. A few orange and purple sconces are the only illumination. This darkness feels placental, as if we are in some marsupial pouch. Shadows as life support. The room is powdered with intelligence; the patients are awake. You can feel their eyes on you, even if you can't see them. Orderlies are now going from bed to bed, bending over the lumpy shadows that I know will turn into people, when our eyes adjust. Administering shots. "Dusking" them. Knocking these people out, at their request.

This is the latest med-slang for the electives' group sedation, explains Dr. Glasheen to Justine Harkonnen. Dr. Glasheen has usurped me as the chaperone. He walks us to Bed One. Arm in arm, the Harkonnens follow him while I trail behind, walking pigeon-toed to hush the squeaking of my soles.

The first elective we meet is a black woman in her late forties, Genevieve Hughes. Upon seeing Dr. Glasheen, her entire face changes. After a second, she manages a thin smile. Politeness overrides the gleam of terror in her eyes. But I gather from the reaction of other electives around us that the tall doctor must inspire this reflexive fear wherever he goes on Ward Seven, which makes sense given his role here: Dr. Glasheen, the Sleep Enforcer, King of Needles.

Genevieve Hughes's eyes are like empty bowls that you want to fill with food. How has she lost so much weight and hair already? At home, she says, it got to where she was plucking out her eyelashes to stay awake, even as every cell in her body demanded sleep. Her husband drove her to the hospital. He begged her to enlist in the Ward Seven group sleep-therapy program. "Live," he said. (Hearing this, I feel a pang of, what, envy maybe—because that is one beautifully succinct pitch, Mr. Hughes.) With obvious effort, Genevieve directs a grateful smile at Dr. Glasheen, even as she grips the bed's guardrails with both hands, as if to avoid recoiling further from the man. Without Dr. Glasheen's help, she says, she could not bear to face the dream again.

Before her contagion? Genevieve tells us she runs the downtown cineplex with her husband. We all nod excitedly—everyone present has seen a Saturday matinee at her theater and dreamed in tandem with dozens of other moviegoers. When Dori and I were growing up, this theater was a rat-infested death trap, but the Hugheses have since rehabbed the lobby into an Arabian palace that serves Milk Duds. "Oh!" says

Mr. Harkonnen, pleased. "I know where that place is! My wife, before she was my wife, I took her to your theater, ma'am." And even Dr. Glasheen cracks the brown egg of his face to smile. "I used to love scary movies, myself," says Genevieve, "before the insomnia kicked in." In April, she received the tainted sleep transfusion. Two nights later, the nightmare appeared inside her. Dr. Glasheen is smiling vacantly, checking his watch out of the squeezed corners of his eyes. The Harkonnens are now staring at Genevieve Hughes with frank, unsettled expressions. As she describes her elective insomnia, Genevieve keeps dragging down her lower eyelids with her index fingers, revealing the pink mucosal rims (a common habit among electives, we learn from Dr. Glasheen, who calls his patients, not without affection, "scab-pickers of vision"). She seems unaware that she is doing this. She yawns, sneezes.

"Bless you!" yelp the Harkonnens.

"You cannot catch her nightmare," mouths the doctor to us, in the sort of public whisper that reduces everyone to children. Genevieve looks down at her blanket.

"We know that," says Mr. Harkonnen, in his regular speaking growl.

Then Dr. Glasheen introduces Felix as "Baby A's dad."

Genevieve jumps. Her face blazes with some fever of hope.

"Oh! When we first heard they'd found a cure, my husband and I cried! I'm on the waiting list; they tell me it's another five months yet . . ."

Mr. Harkonnen grunts softly.

Mrs. Harkonnen pulls out mall studio portraits of Baby A to show her. There's Baby A arranged on a stuffed rainbow, a stuffed unicorn, a dirty Pegasus. Apparently, the sadist mall photographer is also some kind of fairy-tale taxidermist. Baby A stares out at us from the wallet-size glossies with her implacable blue eyes.

"And you're the mother?"

"I'm her mother."

The women study each other. Justine's eyes are golf-ball white compared to Genevieve's sunken yellowish ones. The glow produced by the wall sconces seems almost animate, flickering erratically around the room. After Dusking, Dr. Glasheen tells me, they will extinguish even these.

We are all being very disciplined about focusing on Genevieve, and not the other patients around us, some of whom have begun to babble to Dr. Glasheen that they do not want to be sedated, that in fact they would like to be discharged from the hospital.

"After sundown," he complains to me, "they act like *I'm* Donor Y coming for them. They deny they ever requested sedation. I show my patients their signatures on the consents, and they act like it's forgery. Dusking time, and suddenly nobody recognizes their own handwriting."

And this is exactly what happens. Dr. Glasheen excuses himself to help the orderlies. Many of the electives cower at his approach. They seem to develop a spontaneous amnesia, robbed by their foreboding of the Donor Y nightmare of their earlier daylit desire to sleep and live.

Mr. Harkonnen brought a ball cap along just as a stress-prop, it seems. He keeps twisting it in front of his waist, wringing imaginary sweat from the brim. A tear beads in the corner of his eye.

"I hate Donor Y," he says under his breath. "What a monster."

Do you know that I smile? I do. Gotcha, Felix.

Genevieve murmurs something, softer than orange juice sucked through a straw; around us, the Dusking commotion drowns out all sound.

"What's that, Mrs. Hughes?"

We all lean in.

"I don't hate him. I feel terribly, terribly sorry for him, this Donor Y. He had to see these things alone, for who knows how long?"

Genevieve shakes her head, with that strangely paternalistic attitude the sick sometimes take toward the healthy, as if she's preemptively forgiving us for what we're too young to understand. Youth being gauged in this chamber as distance from the Donor Y nightmare. Then she's gone.

All around us, people are exiting the room. Their bodies stay visible, but their eyes flutter and shut. Dusked, they lean back against the blue sheets. Many scream before they vanish. They claw at Dr. Glasheen. And I'm thinking, *Control yourselves, we're watching*. And I'm thinking: *Doctors, are you hearing this? Adjust the goddamn medication*. And I, too, am shaking, with an out-of-nowhere anger. Not until the entire bedroom has gone quiet do I relax my grip on Justine's arm. Mr. Harkonnen has got her other hand.

Some electives clench and grind their jaws with closed eyes, giving them a constipated look.

Some take on a magenta cast, as though their skin is being glazed from within by a barbecue brush—fluctuating body temperature, says the unworried orderly. Dr. Glasheen is explaining something to us about the physiological differences between natural versus induced sleep, although nobody is paying attention. His hands, I notice as he gestures at their bodies, look big enough to juggle pumpkins. I wonder what he dreams about, off-shift. I wonder if he wouldn't like to lift his patients' scalps and scoop the terrible vision out of them. Mr. Harkonnen and Mrs. Harkonnen are frowning down at the vacated faces on the pillows like parents at a swim meet, trying to glimpse the divers' bodies under the froth of bubbles as they glide away.

"She won't enter REM sleep for another ninety minutes," he tells them.

Mrs. Harkonnen's blue eyes are shining wet.

Mr. Harkonnen says, "There ought to be some way to arm them, you know. Send them back into this asshole's nightmare with a handgun, some protection. It's not fair."

"It's not fair," agrees Dr. Glasheen, with the worn-smooth voice of someone whose notions of justice have all been filed away by the nightly emery of his hospital duties.

In the last bed, a woman has somehow managed to Houdini out of the elastic beige restraints and her green paper gown. Now she's lying naked on top of the sheets, snoring lightly. She's fallen asleep on her back with her pale feet crossed at the ankles. A fine sweat glistens all over her body, so that she looks like a melting icicle.

DONOR Y

Four a.m., the morning after Ward Seven.

Can't sleep. Can't sink into sleep.

My diet of zeros doesn't seem to be working anymore.

Something else to hate you for, Donor Y.

BABY A

I want to learn Baby A's name.

This desire has been growing in me for days now, spiking with the Donor Y crisis, and tonight I feel crazed with it—actually, feverish. Donors under the age of eighteen are assigned a letter at random, an "Alpha-Nym," by our system. Most parents slip up at some point, blurt out their child's full name. Not the Harkonnens. "Baby A," they say smoothly, tucking her identity into this blanket. Mrs. Harkonnen may well have told me her daughter's name at our first meeting in the grocery store parking lot, but I didn't know to pay attention back then.

As crazy as it sounds, I keep feeling that if I knew her true name, I could protect her better. I've heard strangers refer to "Baby A" as if she is some inorganic compound, a designer sleep drug. All night, people dial the hotline and beg me to get them wait-listed for the "Baby A cure." Anyone in America who has a bad dream calls in, which means the phones never stop ringing. I go hoarse shouting down their doubts: "No," I say, "the helmet is safe, the tubes are sterilized. No, there is zero chance that you will contaminate the nation's sleep supply, as he did." I promise my recruits that the Donor Y crisis has precipitated important policy changes, exhaustive safety rubrics for the Sleep Vans, expensive rounds of testing for nightmare prions. All this public paranoia, I say, obscures the statistics: sleep donation has never been safer.

I don't feel great about this, myself.

"How *do* we really know it's safe for these people to donate?" I ask Jim and Rudy.

"We don't know."

"We can't know."

"That kind of epistemic murk is unavoidable, Edgewater."

"Error, of course, is inevitable in some proportion of the cases."

"We should describe the Donor Y tragedy as a freakish exception—which it is."

"But it's unrealistic to expect perfection from any human institution, Trish."

"And from any human, period."

"You know this."

Boy, do I.

"We need to accept the world as it is, honey, not as we wish it to be," Jim says, with a self-regarding puff on the *wish* and the *be*. Jim, I'm told, was a theater major at his Midwestern college. He often projects these Page-a-Day aphorisms from his diaphragm, as if he were still auditioning to be Jean Valjean in *Les Mis*.

But the need is quantifiable, uncontestable, and growing. People are drowning in light, fully awake. Children are propped on pillows, foaming soft sounds, singing a terrible music without words. We show videos of them at drives, which get incredible sleep-yields. Moms who see it are ready to strip down in the nearest Sleep Van and give us five years of sleep on the spot. Some of the youngest orexins became insomniacs at age two; they have no memories of sleeping. Cued by some off-screen producer, these obliging, dying toddlers tell the large blank eye of the camera that they do not remember dreaming one night in their lives. Sleep: What is that?

These children live in a state of conscious terror, their school days exchanged for a noon-lit netherworld. The sleep banks in Virginia, Florida, and Oregon are dried out. So I keep calling.

At a little after midnight, my voice gives out. The office trailer is equipped with a Murphy bed, what I think of as the whipped cream of beds, sprouting whitely from the wall. I pull it down.

"Working late?"

It's just me and Jeremy in here now. Everyone else left hours ago.

Jeremy is our Mobi-Van's shy secretary, biracial, not quite thirty, who wears his hair in a carroty Afro and has dozens of chunky rings and ear cuffs and basically looks like a warlock in denim. He has what I suppose you might call "boundary issues" in a healthier office environment; here, he's just one open eye among many. His reward for being an extraordinarily effective person is that he does the equivalent of three jobs for the same low salary. Jeremy is a sweetheart. He looks our recruits in their eyes when he thanks them, and piles wool blankets near the feet of the unconscious donors. When the nurses start a draw, he flinches for them. He donates sleep himself. Since the crisis began, Jeremy's given half a year of his life: 4,392 hours—he grins proudly—which is far in excess of the legal limits; Rudy or Jim must be pulling strings for him to give so much, on a regular basis. Somebody needs to cut him off now. If you give beyond your sleep-recharge threshold, push beyond the body's natural limits, you'll suffer the same consequences of sleep loss that afflict our insomniacs: cognitive impairment, physiological exhaustion, collapse. Jeremy stumbles around the trailer like a zombie some mornings, zonked from a nine-hour draw.

I realize that he is hovering in front of the door, glancing back at me with a look that is totally unlike Jeremy, full of cagey apprehensiveness.

"You're sleeping here?"

"I am."

"Want a tuck-in?"

I do.

"Just let me brush my teeth," I mumble.

He hits the lights.

It's been years since I've done anything resembling ordinary socializing. For most of my colleagues at the Corps, this is so. We joke that the Insomnia Crisis has ruined our sex lives—we don't have time to sleep with anyone recreationally, we're too busy begging for sleep on the phone.

I listen under the sheets as Jeremy unzips his jeans near the door, wriggles out of them. Tiny wood-sprite eyes litter the darkness, red and green—just the office electronics. No true darkness left in the modern world, some Luddites complain, fingering light pollution as the root of the new insomnia. Jeremy, a wiry shadow, lowers his full weight onto the Murphy, which whinnies on its springs; this Murphy bed turns out to be an expert ventriloquist of eager naked bodies. He gives me a nip on my bare neck. Then a consulting kiss, salty and quick. Jeremy's hands, which are so warm, move under my clothing with a confidence that suggests he has been in touch with some of our colleagues about my amenability.

One thing the Corps has taught me is that my needs are quite common. I have become much more forthright about disclosing them. Shameless, I guess you could say, although I still have a vestige of girlhood modesty, and would prefer the word *honest*. And I am perfectly willing to make a gift-in-kind to my peers, when their complementary need arises. After-hours Jeremy turns out to be a very different quantity than the quiet male secretary who brings baby carrots for lunch and sneezes in sunlight. He, too, is suddenly quite candid about what his body requires from my body. This is our training. Most of our time is spent asking strangers for donations.

There are, of course, no consent forms to sign for this kind of transfusion. No nurses to adjust the fit or monitor its progress.

"Perhaps there is some equivocation on the part of the lady?" Jeremy says at one point, with a frightfully sad tact.

"No, no, I—this is as wet as things ever really get, honey," I whisper. "Under these conditions . . ."

I slide my hips forward on the mattress. After that, we manage beautifully, this hungry silhouette who is my friend Jeremy and I.

"Sorry," he sighs afterward, licking our sweat from my neck. "That was too quick."

I shake my head—it wasn't. Any longer would have been, for me, an almost unbearable exposure to the self-eradicating bliss of servicing and being serviced, all at once. It's a rare transfer wherein both bodies get to be donor and recipient and recipient and donor. We are stroking each other's knuckles now, side by side on the Murphy.

Jeremy sits up and swings his legs over the bed's edge. He doubles over into a faceless hill, feeling around the floor for the shed skins of his socks, his T-shirt.

"Stay?" I blurt out.

This in stark violation of the contract.

"Oh, God, Trish, I—"

"No, sorry, I'm not thinking clearly, it's gotten so late. Go"—I hand him his missing sock, give a little push—"you need a good night's sleep."

Jeremy cocks his head at me for a confusing moment; then he squeezes my hand and stands, hobbles toward the trailer exit.

"Thank you," we say at the same time, and my whole body heats up.

"Get some rest, girl."

After I hear his car drive off, I turn the lights back on.

You know, I'm afraid that working for the Corps may be irreversibly perverting the way I evaluate human exchanges. *Now* who is the donor, the donee? I'll wonder, watching a high school couple kiss at the mall. Are they a match? Will their transfusion be a success? What songs are the corporations piping into her body? I'll ask myself on the city bus, watching the driver's long neck tense and relax as she receives rhythm transfusions via her fuchsia earbuds.

The Storches' "office" within the trailer is a locked shed on wheels annexed to the main vehicle. It's a wonder that the two inventors of ergonomic johns can function in such a comfortless space.

Quite easily, with the key I copied two years ago, I enter Jim and Rudy's inner sanctum. It smells like Pine-Sol and cinnamon chewing gum.

On my knees, I go sleuthing for her records.

"Harkonnen, Baby A——"

The Storches keep hard copies of important documents in an old-school filing cabinet, school-locker gray, the ichthyosaur of the modern storage world. ("Everything is, of course, also in the cloud," I've overheard Rudy reassuring visitors, which is a very disorienting and mystical statement, out of context.)

Hunting her name, I come across a stack of letters addressed to Jim. On impulse I read one. I read the whole batch. They are more frightening to me than the Donor Y nightmare. I read through them twice, my eyes blurring and uncrossing; I feel a funny pang, imagining Jeremy home in his bed. It's three a.m. Who am I supposed to call now? I lift the phone to dial the Harkonnens, hang it back on the receiver. I stare at Dori's photographs on the Slumber Corps pamphlets, a stack of hundreds, and start to cry.

JIM

....

The following morning, Jim calls me into his office. How much can you age in one day? Wrinkles I've never seen before are now tractor-gouged across his forehead. We stare across his desk, his gray eyes regarding mine with a strange calm: It's a gaze that feels prehistoric, entirely shorn of seven years of respect and affection. I stare back. For just a moment, I get this aerial sense of what might happen next, like the view from the top of the roller coaster. This is power, I realize. Not just seeing the future, but deciding it. Jim's career is in my hands.

Then Jim surprises me by speaking first.

"So. Who are you planning to tell?"

All night, I rehearsed for this confrontation. I'd assumed that, as Jim's accuser, I would lead.

"Who told you that I know?"

"Cameras, Trish. You don't think we have cameras in here?"

Cameras? Blood rushes to my face.

"You saw what we—what Jeremy and I . . ."

Horrifyingly, Jim grins.

At dawn I'd stripped the Murphy bed and folded it back into the wall; the sticky sheets are bunched in a bag at my feet, to be smuggled out of the trailer after sunset. I wonder how many of the dozens of donations I've taken and offered on the Murphy bed have been witnessed by Jim, or Rudy.

"Jim, I'm sorry," I hear myself apologizing. "I shouldn't have gone through your things—"

"We trusted you."

"I only wanted to know Baby A's name—"

"My God, Trish. I would have told you that." Jim, who is never angry, is fury-mottled, his entire neck cheetah print. "Now look what you've done—you've threatened our entire organization."

Her name is Abigail. Abby Harkonnen. I'm not the only one who knows this. A biotech firm in Japan has been purchasing units of her sleep from Jim, for a dollar sum that left me reeling. Jim's first correspondence with them is dated a mere two weeks after Baby A's inaugural donation; most of the catch from her third and fourth draws was sold to a Tokyo lab. It's unclear from the letters who else might have been involved, or how Jim managed to smuggle her sleep out of the country. I have no idea what, if anything, Rudy might know; these letters were signed by Jim. According to one contract I found, assuming I read the thing right, Jim has made in excess of fifty million dollars for the sale of Baby A's sleep.

How dare you—I know this is a moral anachronism. A phrase sad and silly, excerpted from an era of bygone incredulity, from a black-and-white movie; and yet for hours last night, alone on the Murphy bed, these were the only three words I could think.

"So now we have a real problem, Trish."

He gives me a stern look, as if I'm the one in trouble.

"Jim?" My voice comes out in a child's whisper. "Why did you do this?"

"Their team approached me. They'll clone her sleep before we manage it, I guarantee it. They are working to make an artificial injectable right this second."

"All that money—"

"Went right back into our organization. Nothing traceable to us, or to the Harkonnen baby. Anonymous donations," he says smoothly, and I don't know whether to believe him.

"But the Harkonnens," I try again. *Jim? Where have you gone?* What I want, impossibly, is to blow the whistle on Jim *to* Jim; to appeal to my "real" boss, who would surely be appalled to learn what this doppelgänger monster who has stolen Jim Storch's face and name has done.

"We're not hurting anybody, baby." Now he's speaking in the soothing voice I love, the voice of yesterday-Jim, as if responding to my mental summons. Somehow this familiar tone makes me feel much worse. Queasily, I stare at my hands splayed on Jim's desk.

"Only a portion of her donations has gone overseas. The rest, as you know better than anybody, we've distributed in this country."

I'm grinding down so hard my jaw is pulsing. *An artificial injectable.* How much money does he stand to gain, I wonder, if the Japanese team succeeds?

He tries a different tack.

"Trish, weren't you and Dori raised religious? Do you know

the parable of the loaves and the fishes? The mustard seed, the parable of the talents?"

When he sees my blank face, he shrugs.

"Forget it. We grew up Irish Catholic. Look: I took the Harkonnen gift, and I *multiplied it*. Can you imagine what it will make possible if they synthesize her sleep? In the grand scheme, the benefits that accrue to every living person will be extraordinary."

My head has been shaking *no*, I realize, possibly since this conversation began.

"But I've been telling her parents that her draws go straight to the National Sleep Bank. That we need every drop of her sleep to save lives—"

"So you know," he snaps, as if he's lost his patience with a delinquent student. "Who do you plan to tell?"

"Jim. We have to—"

Now it's my turn to pause, self-startled. From the lump in my throat, I discover that I am unready to separate from our "we," not yet, or to evict Jim from that pronoun. For seven years, we've been a team. And Jim loves my sister, not just what she does for our organization, I feel very certain of that.

"Did you keep some of the money?" I hear myself ask.

"Listen, Trish, we cannot control for every variable. Human greediness . . . it's not even necessarily a bad thing, in my opinion."

Jim seems to round some bend in his own mind; without warning, like the sun breaking through clouds, he is smiling almost wistfully down his long nose at me.

"Maybe it's just what we mean when we say a necessary evil. Look at the population we serve. Any one of the insomniacs, at any time, could choose death. Some do, as you know. The ones who get their name on our waiting lists want to sleep because they want to live. They are greedy, greedy, greedy for relief, more life."

Jim is a better recruiter than Rudy. I watch his gray eyes go mock ingenuous behind his glasses. He quits trying to bully me.

"It's your choice, of course." He steeples his long fingers, his smile now one of rueful contemplation. I can no longer tell what is genuine, what is performance; perhaps Jim shares my confusion.

"Jim—"

"I'm just urging you to think about the consequences of your actions. *My* life will be over, of course—it will kill me, frankly, the scandal. But let's not talk about my life; that's quite irrelevant to the big picture. Instead, Trish, I'd suggest you think about the suffering people on our waiting lists. The media will be all over us. Look at the disruption from Donor Y, the damage *he's* caused!"

I nod.

"The fines will be astronomical. Our public image will never fully recover. Without the goodwill of the public, what do we run on? Trish, I know that you are smart enough to understand why it was necessary to give these foreign researchers a crack at achieving synthesis. But the media is going to crucify me, they don't give a damn who they hurt, and listen, there will be a run on the sleep banks like something out of the Great Depression. People will die, no doubt. Laws might be overturned—infant donations could become a thing of the past. We will certainly never draw from Baby A again if you turn me in."

"What if you just . . . confess, Jim. Apologize, resign."

Jim shakes his head at me so slowly, with a maddening air,

affectionate and severe, like some fairy-tale father denying his daughter a poisoned apple.

"I know that would make things more comfortable for *you*."

"Please, Jim," I say, hating and hating the meekness of my voice. This is not how I imagined our confrontation going. "Please, will you turn yourself in? I don't want to be the one."

He takes off his glasses, rubs his eyes, puts the glasses on again.

"So you've convinced yourself, then. You've already decided. You think it's *the right thing to do*, regardless of the cost to millions of terminally ill people."

"I didn't say that . . ."

I can feel my uncertainty returning, a thickening blue mist that rolls in between Jim's face and my own. Helplessly, I watch this happen. Then my decision softens back into a speculation: What will happen to the Corps, and to all the people on our waiting lists, if I fail to keep Jim's confidence? He's right, isn't he? We are still in crisis mode from Donor Y; easily, I can imagine a nationwide boycott of the sleep banks if the news about an infant's "stolen sleep" breaks. I can imagine much worse.

And nobody else is doing this work.

"No, you're bound and determined to sink us, are you? Tie up the Corps in another bullshit scandal."

"Jim—"

"So." He leans back in his chair. "When are you going to tell them?"

"Who?"

"The Harkonnens."

DONOR Y

Breaking news: the Donor Y nightmare appears to have provoked a mass suicide. Early reports indicate that between the hours of midnight and two a.m., eleven women woke and dressed and left their houses. Insect-synced by the dreadful coincidence of their illness, by a motive foreign to their formerly healthy minds, they embarked on a nocturnal migration to the coastline. This plot was smuggled into them by the Donor Y nightmare, swear the victims' grieving families. They were not driving at all but driven by his vision. At one bridge near San Rafael, the women queued up, only women that night, according to police reports; they jumped in the fuzzy glow of their headlights, their cars still idling behind them, sliding out of their slippers or stepping out of their heels, climbing barefoot up the girders, taking ginger, seaward steps along the black rail, trailing shadows. There is footage of them falling, captured by a useless security camera riveted to the bridge pilings. Gulls sometimes flit past the camera lens, shrieking, and it is hard to see these birds and not to think of the ghosts of the infected women.

BABY A

....

The suburbs are rain-wet and green. Those white flowers look even more abundant than before, if that's possible. They could be sentient, almost, wagging their lunar tongues at us from glittering gutters and construction sites. The van pulls around a familiar corner, parks. The moon really is inexpressibly bright.

Does it matter if we mean what we say, if the mere fact of the utterance saves lives? I am thinking about Jim, what to do about him.

Tonight, Baby A's blue eyes flutter open in the catch-crib; a nurse adjusts the flow of the ultrasedative, and she falls into REM sleep within seconds. It's a free fall, accelerated by our medications; she descends through the uppermost levels into deep sleep, our monitors confirming "delta wave," and it's from this vacant corridor of being, beyond the reach of language, image, or memory, that Abigail Harkonnen produces the life-saving black flow, the cure for insomnia, sleep piped in from her last home, perhaps, whatever "stasis in darkness" precedes even the womb.

After the draw is done, I bike straight home. It's a little after one a.m. I've locked the bike and I'm heading to the apartment when I notice headlights come on at the end of the street. A car rolls slowly toward me, blinding me. A brown sedan with turquoise doors.

"Get in," says Mr. Harkonnen. "We're going on a field trip."

NIGHT WORLD

Night Worlds, in some regions of America, are now referred to as "Eyesores." Apparently, not even terminal insomniacs can resist the urge to pun. A sign is visible from the highway: ALL SORE-EYES WELCOME!

In our county, the Night World is located at the exit for the old fairgrounds, which have been converted into a midnight solarium. A sapphire penumbra rings the entire complex of tents and shanties. After a silent twenty minutes, Mr. Harkonnen parks in an overgrown field; he walks around and opens my door. He steers me, holding tight to the flesh of my upper arm; for balance, I grab hold of his wrist. His thick fingers around my arm feel like a blood pressure cuff. We moth along toward the light in this odd physical arrangement, swinging our free arms. Dozens of jalopies and motorcycles have been abandoned here, their chrome-plated wheels swallowed in the weeds like jewel-toned ruins. Some of these are luxury vehicles: BMWs, Jaguars. There is something perversely cheering to me about the fact that tonight, rich insomniacs must have gotten lonely enough to disable their alarms and leave their marble enclaves, coming down the mountain to a Night World.

Two months after the Donor Y contagion, there are those who need sleep and those who fear it. If there is friction between these two terminal camps—envy, resentment, suspicion—I don't feel it. *Celebration* is definitely the wrong word for what we're seeing: the pack of slack, exhausted bodies, leaning on silver fenders. But I hear laughter. True hoots and back-claps. Little-bird sounds of cheeks kissed in greeting. It's what you might call a heterogeneous mix of revenants (and I think for some reason of our great-aunt's AA meetings, the weak greenish light and hurt savage smiles, decades-sober alcoholics and freckled young drunks gathered in a church basement around a coffeepot). Old orexins, new electives. Have these faces been awake for days, weeks, months? Years? It's a surprisingly tough call. *Insomnia ages you overnight*—this is a new Oil of Olay cliché minted by the beauty industry, which is really pushing those day-to-night creams now. We pass four girls in a huddle who could be sisters. Those *eyes*. Wound-tight flesh. Hair in strings. Cyan networks of veins around their temples, like some cruel Greek crown. Teeth eroded to a monochrome gray. Three black girls, one ghost-white girl. Electives, infected with the Donor Y nightmare, I'd guess, given what we overhear:

"Look, if you do fall asleep? You gotta try to stay *awake* inside the dream."

People are symptoms of dreams—

This was our favorite line of poetry, my sister's and mine, in the lone college class we'd ever taken together, before her professors finally united to insist that she take a medical leave of absence. Dori picked it out, from Fanny Howe's *O'Clock*, and let me tag along in the wake of her mature aesthetic. It was a generous hand-me-down, her taste in poetry; she also gave me her favorite green leather jacket, her Fender Starcaster, and the leftovers of her beauty products. I was the heiress to all the unused crazy colors in her eye shadow three-packs, you know, the freak blue Maybelline smuggles in between the taupe and the gray, which Dori always said was like the strawberry you're forced to buy in Neapolitan ice cream; plus Dori's prostitute-on-holiday blusher, Dori's pressed powder that looked like ancient silicate from *Planet of the Apes*. I threw it all away after her death, which I now have come to regret. Words I guess are her more durable artifacts. Only how did the rest of our poem go?

> *People are symptoms of dreams*
> *Bombs are symptoms of rage*

Dori, with her ancient face at twenty: "It's a real mind-fuck. I won't be beautiful again, will I?" And before I could answer, "Shut up, shut up, shut up. I'm sorry. That was a shitty thing to ask. Don't lie. Trish? Let's get the mirrors out of here, okay?"

Mr. Harkonnen and I pass the group of teenage girls. We fall in step with an older crowd. Veterans, I'm assuming. LD-ers with the telltale features: desolated eyes and cheek hollows, nacreous skin. The Night World is a ten-minute walk west of here. I remember this hike from grade school; yellow school buses had parked and spilled kids into these same fields. Mr. Harkonnen and I are moving at twice the speed of the insomniacs around us. I'm tempted to stagger, fake a limp. Out of some misguided solidarity? To protect these sick ones from my health? Sometimes, at Sleep Drives, I will catch myself unconsciously adopting the accent of the immigrant family I'm recruiting, mangling my own English, falling in step with the foreign family's rhythms. In any case, Mr. Harkonnen won't let me fall back. He races us along.

The boardwalk is only lit at intervals. Wide orange planks alternate with stripes of raw night. Fifty yards ahead of us, shadows acquire gender, features, then slide back into anonymity. We step onto the wooden platform and walk through a cracked neon rainbow that buzzes twelve feet above us. It's the old entrance to the county fair. A relic from more innocent times, pre–Night World, resuscitated by some insomniac electrician. Now a grim arcade spills before us: stalls that advertise midnight barbers, disbarred sleep doctors, bartender-pharmacists. Dark green and purple tents ripple across the grass like Venus flytraps, their bright flaps swallowing people. Kiosks hawk antidotes to thought, to light:

BEST QUALITY LULLABIES

OBLIVION PRODS

DR. BOB BRAIN'S HATCHET—
CUT THE ELECTRICITY ONCE AND FOR ALL

The boardwalk unwinds for seeming miles, and I know from adolescent explorations that eventually these fairgrounds dissolve into a true woods, a nature preserve of spruce and pines.

When I tell Mr. Harkonnen that this is my first visit to a Night World, he is unaccountably pleased.

We draw up to one of the speakeasy tents.

The chalkboard lists the evening specials.

Medicines, a thousand of them, to induce sleep.

Medicines to *stay awake*—sunlight bulleting through an elective insomniac's brain.

"In here," says Mr. Harkonnen. "Ladies first."

It's very easy, I discover, to comply with him. Since strapping into his sedan, I've felt unworthy of objecting to anything that's happening. Once the tent's flaps close, I find myself crowding as near as I can comfortably get to Mr. Harkonnen's sweat-damp left side. What a crowd. Near the flaps, a trio of twenty-somethings are sharing a pint of some dubious medicine. Tangerine bubbles fizz over the rim. Bubbles are rising in every glass in the joint, Mr. Harkonnen points out, marine blue and dark pink and lurid violet. So these aren't your standard soda mixers, but some self-catalyzing enchantment. Threads of limber color rise to meet the insomniacs' parched lips, as if, inside their pint glasses, these medicines are already doing the work of dreaming for them. Up and down the wooden bar, insomniacs sit a breath away from one another on the high, rickety stools. The way they booze as a unit makes me think of Vikings rowing a longship. Lifting their glasses, slamming them down. Fighting the waves, I assume, inside their bodies.

Sink-and-Swim is the name of one of the advertised soporifics.

But the bartender-pharmacist keeps splashing grapey black and auroral fluids into alternating glasses, and you get the sense some tide is truly turning. In this Night World, the two groups are generating their own countercurrent. They laugh, gulp, swallow, they even seem to blink, to one rhythm.

I doubt it's my right, as a healthy sleeper, to read the scene this way and to be enchanted by the Night World's unlikely friendliness; but I am anyhow.

The footage I best remember, from local television depictions: This same fairground looked like a refugee camp. Dozens of bone-thin bodies swarming the bonfires, flumes of red flame in metal cans, their shoulder bones jutting rhythmically through the free blankets from the Night World dispensary, like big cats gathered around a kill.

Next to us, a woman's head is rolling on a man's shoulder, her pink curls tumbling onto his chest like a cloud at anchor. I think she's an elective whom Donor Y infected. Her eyes are milky and ewe-blank, hugely dilated; she jumps when she yawns. "Keep me up," she demands, and this scarecrow of a man bellies around on the barstool to face her, tucking his shirt into his waistband; obligingly, he strokes her moist forehead, the strawberry rash on her cheeks and chin, the cuticle-width scar under her left eye. Trying to keep her in this world with him, awake. He's an orexin, I think—someone who wants only to sleep—and he's not looking so hot himself: eggy eyes, poached by his illness; skin like white wax. On a calendar, I bet these two are in their early thirties. The whole time his fingers brush her pimpled hairline, he's murmuring something into her earlobe, like her face is a story he's reading to her. Her Braille memoir. He reads on, and with each syllable, her smile widens. With his big thumbs, he prizes her eyelids open. This he does for the exhausted, terrified woman with a clinical tenderness and focus—one species of sufferer trying to help another. I'm holding my breath. The man catches me watching, winks.

Are they a couple? I ask.

The man smiles.

"Sure. Met her five minutes ago, when I sat down here. You're invited to the wedding."

Recipients and donors. Donors and recipients. Variations of this couple's exchange are happening with a hothouse spontaneity up and down the bar: people with equal but opposite afflictions, propping each other up.

This is my beautifully stable impression of Night World culture for maybe two more minutes; then something explodes near my head. Blue medicine leaks in an Arctic smear down the cabinet door. Whatever it is smells faintly of garlic. So much for romance. Near the tent flaps, a fight has broken out: two gizzardy LD-ers are haggling over their bar tab. It seems they have goaded each other into consuming two thousand dollars' worth of some placebo-slush. They dispute the bill in hoarse screams: "That was *your round*, Leonard!" Napkins wag from their hands, covered in scrawled numbers, two rival accounts of their debts to each other—a bar tab that seems to stretch back to the Big Bang.

Mr. Harkonnen returns with our drinks. To avoid the brawl, we retreat further into the tent, choose stools next to a dark oak cabinet.

"Got us the cheap stuff," he says.

"Okay. Thank you."

Shooting Stars is the name of my medicinal cocktail.

I don't ask what it does. Three sips in, my expectations go colorless. Then I find myself leaning against Mr. Harkonnen's left side. Mr. Harkonnen smells like nothing unexpected: burned coffee grounds, Old Spice aftershave. These odors are like flung harpoons—they sail out of the Night World and back across the highway, wrenching whole continents of normalcy into this dark tent: malls and supermarkets, nonlethal sunsets, jarred tomatoes, orderly hedgerows, carpet cleaner, kitty litter, everybody's junk mail piling up on tables, geese flapping across meridians on their winter-spring cycle . . . and soon I'm having to close my eyes to fight a supreme dizziness, as many times and seasons collide inside my chest. I take another long gulp of the cocktail. This time, the effect is immediate. Heat radiates outward until my skin feels ready to burst, until my skeleton is both holding me upright on the barstool and dissolving, inside me, into melting vertebrae, a million memories unstoppered in my brain, rising up my spine, flowing down, my body too small to contain them, shrinking even as the dizzy light expands in all directions, and no way to protect myself against the assault, this onslaught of sound and light, and nowhere to release it, all the aggregating echoes, Dori's voice, our father's, a thousand other whisperers . . .

I blink twice, rub my eyes: incredibly, the Night World tent is still here. I study my watch, relieved that I can read the numbers: three minutes have elapsed since we sat down. Beside me, Mr. Harkonnen is eating green pistachios out of an ashtray. He smiles at me. His face looks placid, in the illegible and alien way that stingrays' bellies look placid as they smooth along glass walls.

"That was an intense drink," I say, frowning down at my lap.

"Still is."

"Was it supposed to wake us up?"

"You bet."

I rub my tingling ears.

"Are you, ah, feeling it?"

"I'm drinking a virgin medicinal cocktail, actually."

"Oh. So . . ."

"Just gin."

Mr. Harkonnen leans back against the side of the medicine cabinet. His arms are flung gregariously behind his head. I blink down at our shoes, my head still spinning.

"I thought we should have a private talk," he says. "Away from the house."

I gaze up at him from behind my glass. Some disturbed dreamer has scratched *Screams from the raven-lunged* in a vitreous green ink on the wooden bar. The tent's droning moonlamps make it feel as though we're all boozing inside a tremendous bug zapper.

"Things have become tense," he adds. "Around the household."

"You're fighting with Justine?"

"We're fighting, yes."

"About Baby A?"

"No, about the recycling. What do you think?"

He tips his drink back, motions for me to follow suit.

"We were a happy couple, a happy family. Can you imagine that? Six months ago, that was our status: happy. But then you show up—"

"You can stop."

"Oh, she won't hear of it now. 'Divorce me, then,' she says. 'Take me to court. We're going to cooperate with them, it's *the right thing to do.*'"

"It's a donation." I swallow. "Nobody can force you."

"So she thinks—ha!"

Mr. Harkonnen has finished his virgin sleep cocktail. Angrily, he shakes the drained glass.

His tongue darts around to catch the last clear droplets. The tongue's froggy orbit around the glass seems many evolutionary leaps removed from the wounded intelligence in Mr. Harkonnen's black eyes.

"She thinks that one day *you will stop asking.*"

"But we will! When the neuroscientists figure out a way to synthesize what Baby A produces naturally—"

"Ha!"

For the duration of his laughing fit, Mr. Harkonnen stares down at the bar with the bulge-eyed consternation of a man trying to discreetly cough up a bone into a cloth napkin; eventually, he regains control of his voice.

"And how old will my daughter be then?" he asks calmly. "Ten? Twenty?"

She'll be dead. This thought is nothing I will. It blows into and through me, part of a leaf-swirl of my worst fears. To erase it, I imagine Baby A at eighteen, laughing, a bright-eyed college freshman. In my mind's eye she is Dori's age in her last photograph, with Dori's sly smile. Will Baby A graduate? I wonder. Live to a decade that my sister never got to see? Will the crisis go into remission? I try to summon an image of Baby A in middle age, sleeping without the suctioning hiss of our machines, dreaming of something unspeakably beautiful. But I can't seem to nudge the picture any deeper into the future.

"She'll be a lot younger than ten, I bet. The scientists are working around the clock—"

Mr. Harkonnen snaps for the bartender.

"We'd like to try one of your specials."

"Of course. What is your desired State of Vigilance? Or Depth of Sleep?" asks the bartender-pharmacist.

"Sleep for us, this time—"

The bartender-pharmacist winks at Mr. Harkonnen. With her tiny, fox-perfect teeth, she tears a blank envelope.

Service is democratic, I gather, in a Night World. Nobody here prescreens, or hands around eligibility questionnaires. The bewigged bartender-pharmacist, smoothing her magenta bangs, is happy to take our money. Eighty-four dollars for two drinks. Purple powder seems to levitate inside the dark glass, coagulating into tiny continents.

"You'll be out cold," I observe to Mr. Harkonnen. He grins at a dim corner of the tent.

"So will you, though. Bottoms up."

My body tenses, anticipating a second onrush of light. But three sips in, and this time I feel like a bone on sand, powdery and solid, too, and very still. Some protection is in the process of repealing itself. This is scary at first, but soon its absence feels like a relief. The heaviness of sentience, heavy history and caution—the drink drains it away. Shards are winking on the sand inside me, and I find I have no desire to collect them, to dig or to investigate. I am strangely unbothered by the parched bar, the evaporating sea of reason, the flecks of thoughts, their disconnection.

"This is a good one." Mr. Harkonnen says. "Sort of limey. Do you taste lime?"

It doesn't last too long, that first hit of the soporific. A second later, I sober up; the waves come back, and I'm myself again, thinking my thoughts, albeit in a dangerously relaxed state.

Somehow it seems we're talking about Baby A.

"I manage the YMCA. Soccer, baseball. For every boy, there is a season. I wanted a boy, until she came." He smiles down at the bar, squeezing his fists together; it's a funny gesture, and I wonder if he's keeping something for or from himself. "And then I forgot that I ever wanted different."

Until who came?

"Abigail!" I blurt out.

Mr. Harkonnen lifts an eyebrow.

"Baby A," I correct, looking down.

"You got privileges, huh? Teacher's pet? What else do you know about us?"

"I'd never betray her real name to anybody, sir."

"So we're back to 'sir' now."

He takes a long drink.

"Go ahead. Call her Abby. Make her a baby."

His grin hardens until his face looks wind-chapped.

"Baby A—that always sounded to me like some damn sports drink."

I'm scared, and I think he is, too. Light from the moonlamps is reflected in Mr. Harkonnen's eyes, tiny weather vanes spinning in each black pupil, and returning his stare I am dizzily aware that our night could go in any number of directions.

"What did your boss tell me? The tall one—who's that again?"

"Jim. Or Rudy. They're twins. 'Tall' doesn't narrow it down."

"He said you got the highest number of recruits."

I feel myself darken. "Thanks to my sister. Her story."

"So that's the game, huh? You franchise your sister."

"I don't want to talk about her here."

But his eyes gleam, he is taken by this idea.

"Sure. I get it now. You franchise her pain. Dori Edgewater. Well, it worked, didn't it?" He grins at me with slack, fish-pale lips. "She's famous. Everybody knows her, your sister. Just like everybody knows my daughter."

Two hunchbacked men are fighting in the corner with their barstools lifted over their heads, the chair legs facing outward like spiny antlers, so that they look like enormous beetles charging each other. Night World bouncers in their ominous uniforms arrive to break it up. Jacked electives, reports the bartender-pharmacist. This altercation happens in the shallows, near the flaps. At our depth of the speakeasy, nobody so much as blinks.

I wait for Mr. Harkonnen to accuse me now:

You do what he did, he'll add, *to them. You are just like Donor Y.*

Or what else might he say, regarding Dori?

She's dead. She's dead. What's it going to take? Do you want me to ice a cake with that? Your sister's dead. Everything you've done, you've done for yourself alone.

But Mr. Harkonnen's focus seems to have rolled inward, onto his own failures:

"Justine is too damn good for her own good. She has no defenses. And Abby? Poor kid, I'm sure she'll take after her mother. Assuming she makes it out of preschool. You think I can protect either of them, from what they turned out to be? My wife is a far better person than I am. That's why I married her."

I open my mouth intending to agree with him—to compliment the virtue of Mrs. Harkonnen.

Then I think I have my own hiccup of insight into Mr. Harkonnen's dilemma. He got more goodness than he bargained for, maybe, when he married her. Some flood he cannot dam or drain or control. Unfortunately for Felix Harkonnen, we at the Corps have also discovered the same currents of goodness that originally drew him to his wife.

"I'd better shut up," he says after a while. "Drank too much."

But a minute later, he grabs my arm.

"Tell me this," says Felix, whose first name I've yet to say aloud. "If your sister—Dori—were alive today, and she were the universal donor? What would you do, huh? How much would you let them take from her?"

"If it was me, sir, I promise you, I'd let them—"

"But say it's not you, in this scenario. Say it's Dori."

I don't answer.

To our left, there is a burst of muted applause; people are whispering that an orexin woman is genuinely asleep. Two men have lifted her up, and with infinite care they are transporting her through the smoky speakeasy. It's quite something: the crowd falls into a silence that pulses with energetic longing, and people move around her dangling feet with the reverence due a new saint. Watching even one woman nod off into sleep has changed the tent's entire atmosphere. Now the air feels almost musky with group credulity, the group's decision to blink an apparition into reality. Her feet wave at us as she is carried from the tent, her entire body limp. If you were a cynic, you might assume this woman was a plant; her stunt-recovery, if that's what we're watching, seems to be very good for business. Medicines miracle around the bar, everyone buying everyone rounds. Nobody talks. Crickets are singing beyond the tent flaps; you can hear them in the silence. At one of the kiosks, they were selling a specially bred cricket with emerald wings as an "organic lullaby-machine." The woman next to me has one in a ruby-tinted jar on the bar, its red legs fiddling away.

Half my drink is gone, I note. Mr. Harkonnen keeps slipping in and out of focus on the barstool. My muscles, they're melting. Tiny knots untwist themselves throughout my body. What I somehow continue not to say:

[We sell your daughter's sleep.]

What would Felix Harkonnen do if he knew this?

Just imagining the conversation makes my gut cramp. How will I pitch it? I'll tell him I had no idea my boss had brokered this sale with the Japanese researchers. I'll emphasize my ignorance; I'll tell him, too, that Jim Storch seems to genuinely believe that the illegal transfer of Abigail's sleep was both justified and necessary. I find that I badly want to defend Jim to

Mr. Harkonnen, to explain that my boss believed he was acting in everyone's best interests, regardless of whether this is true. I want to restate Jim's grandiose, beautiful claims for Mr. Harkonnen. He called his deal the only way forward.

What if Jim's right?

I squeeze shut. Eyes closed, I try to imagine it: Jim's decision in transit. The Baby A sleep units traveling over the Pacific into the right hands, the capable hands of these Tokyo researchers.

If his scheme fails, the Harkonnens need never know. If his scheme works, and they do achieve synthesis, and manufacture artificial sleep, a faucet of unconsciousness, an inexhaustible dream well, "sleep for all," the realized goal, my God, then we've got an outcome straight out of a comic book, or the New Testament: the Harkonnens sacrificed their infant's sleep, Jim Storch took a bold risk, I kept shut, the Japanese team gets her sleep on tap, all the terminal insomniacs are saved, et cetera, et cetera, freed from the chain of endless dependence on their donors. And why not? Why couldn't it happen, just like that? Religions spore out of such stories. Movies starring Denzel Washington are made of far less.

"Slow down. You've got the hiccups."

Mr. Harkonnen swings an arm around, thumps my back. With his brown hair slicked back like that, with his house-musk of baby powder and Old Spice, and his spatulate hands with their dirty thumbnails, he's got a mammalian sweetness to him in the speakeasy's neon den. His automatic tenderness must come from taking care of Abby. Whenever Mr. Harkonnen burps the baby, he looks like a gentle, enormous beaver. His gesture is well timed with my secret thoughts to make me want to tell him everything; and then, not a second later, to make me scared of losing everyone. Not just Rudy and Jim and my life in the Corps trailer, but the Harkonnens.

I stare at Mr. Harkonnen. A chalky taste rises that I want only to swallow. Easiest to believe Jim's calculations, Jim's predictions. Why not? He has a head for zeroes, Jim. He made his fortune as a businessman.

But it's useless to pretend that I can still trust Jim. Any minute now, I'm going to tell Mr. Harkonnen. As scared as I am, I don't see how it can be avoided. Dori's working in me, on me, dissolving the capsule around the secret. *I must tell you something very upsetting, Mr. Harkonnen . . .*

Will Mr. Harkonnen keep the secret? If I explain to him that the ensuing scandal really could undermine the entire institution? Actually kill people, according to Jim's assessment? I can't imagine that he will respond to the news with silence, or forgiveness.

Mr. Harkonnen is staring at me with a strangely avuncular expression; he hands me a green pistachio, crunches into his own. "There," he says, like everything's settled. "Let's go for a walk. I'd like to show you the Poppy Fields. They're really something. They're way out beyond the tents. Do you know, ever since our field trip to Ward Seven, I've been coming out here every other night. Justine thinks I'm working late. And she's not wrong."

His grin is a further mystification, exposing a black back tooth.

"I am."

"Why?" Then a startling answer occurs to me. "Are you sick, too?"

"No. it's not that. After that night at Ward Seven, I just

wanted to see these people for myself. Solo, you know. Without my wife. Without a chaperone."

I giggle, terrified.

"It's been quite an education."

"For me, too, Mr. Hark—"

"Good. We're just getting started. The night is young."

Something tightens in the air between us and I find that I'm pushing away from the bar, and from the empty glasses and the cracked pistachio hulls and the unslept faces. I have to stand to avoid falling off the barstool. I hold on to the bar's edge, blinking hard into the moonlamps. Felix is studying my eyes. I amend my plan, watching him watching me, or perhaps it is more accurate to say that my plan amends itself, spontaneously inverts: Who is helped, if the father knows about the sale?

No one, says Jim.

Out loud, I make the easier apology:

"About Ward Seven? I'm really, really sorr—"

"Don't!" he roars. When the bartender-pharmacist looks over, he laughs: This is all in good fun, ma'am. He needn't worry. Under her wig, her yellow-brown eyes regard us with a hilted intelligence, halted judgment. All of Night World seems to sparkle with a similar neutrality. Dulled gazes like swords in scabbards. Then we are back on the boardwalk, joining others on their slow bar crawl under the stars.

THE POPPY FIELDS

The Poppy Fields have been widely reported on: a special strain of poppy that releases an "aromatic hypnotic," sometimes called an "olfactory blanket." Poppies are trendy, if that word can be applied to foredoomed miracle cures. All over the country, Night World gardeners are pruning the flame-bright poppies beneath the moon. The gardeners' headlamps reveal a wilderness of faces, insomniacs whose bloodshot eyes are even redder than the poppies. They lie on bedrolls and grain sacks in parallel rows, breathing in the flowers.

We reach the edge of the boardwalk, step off into grass.

In the distance, the woods wall us from the city. Pines span the horizon, nearly black in color at this hour, with the pointy, standard look of fence posts. A wooden sign with an arrow reads: FIFTY YARDS TO THE POPPY FIELDS.

Behind us, the fairgrounds waver like some hallucinatory reef: the calm anemone billowing of the Night World tents, the barkers' poles like red coral, the electric-green spokes of the

Dream Wheel. At this distance, even the screams of the insomniacs receiving Oblivion Prods contribute to this illusion, their faraway cries transformed by repetition into an implacable background, like waves crashing on rocks.

And then we are midcalf in acres of flowers. "The Placebo Fields," we joke in the Mobi-Van—but, my God, it is hard to hold on to your cynicism when you actually see them. Under the moon, the poppies look as bright as jewels on the seafloor. We wade through hundreds of them, the scarlet buds drumming against our shins, and I find it's almost frightening to bend the stems back, to graze the petals with my fingers. This is no mirage. But it's a shock to find this sea at our city's edge, and to find myself navigating it with Mr. Harkonnen. Who knows if the poppies' fragrance is a real insomnia cure? I realize that I don't smell a thing. But my thoughts shrink to a whisper, and soon I start to feel like I'm sleeping already.

Pain tickles my heel.

"I think I stepped on something . . ."

"I'd keep walking," said Mr. Harkonnen, swallowing, his voice a thick buzz in my ears, "if I were you."

"Will you look for me, will you check—"

"It's okay, Trish."

And this is like a birdcall: the sound of my name. Memories spread their wings, come home to roost, and I shudder under the weight of all these Trishes I've been, before the purple sleep cocktail, before the Night World parking lot and before my knock on the door that turned Mr. Harkonnen's daughter into Baby A, before the sleep crisis, and even before Dori's last day.

Very gratefully, I keep pace with him.

Remember this, I instruct myself.

Mr. Harkonnen steers me toward a small shack in the center

of the field. It looks like a boat at anchor in this strange Atlantic. Night World staffers mill around it, grabbing blankets, chatting with groups of insomniacs.

"Do you know about the Legend of the Poppies?" a young attendant asks us, tugging her black ponytail around her collarbone. She is the valet, I realize, taking cash for the bedrolls and the blue inhalers, directing bodies to their pallets among the red flowers.

"I do," says Mr. Harkonnen. "You told me. But tell her."

With the mercenary cheer of any waitress, she beams at us each in turn.

"According to Greek legend, the poppy flower was the gift of Hypnos, the god of sleep, to help Demeter dream again. Demeter was exhausted by the search for her lost daughter, whom Hades had taken to be his bride in the Underworld. Now, Demeter was so tired that she could no longer make the harvest grow. But Hypnos's poppies cast a spell on her. She slept, and when she woke, the corn was growing green and tall again."

Mr. Harkonnen fishes for his wallet, tips her a buck.

"Yup. Thanks. That's a rough night for Mom. The devil's got your daughter."

This valet is a tall Asian woman who looks about the same age as our Slumber Corps interns. She wears a long white coat and a white dress, for "atmosphere maintenance and heightened visibility," she says. Behind her, the wind is picking up. It plows the fields. Each gust forces the worst kind of devotion from the mutely chattering blossoms, grinding them against the soil, knocking their red heads around. The wind could do this to us, too, at any instant, it seems to want us to know, and the thousand poppies nod their agreement.

Suddenly I am overcome by drowsiness.

Mr. Harkonnen, beside me, lets out a shuddering yawn.

Women wander the poppy fields, in white nightgowns, carrying vessels of water, or some other transparent liquid. In calm, emotionless voices, they begin to halt the unsteady pilgrims and to ask them questions:

"Would you like a sip of the supplemental poppy tea, dear?"

"Would you like sheets and a pillow? We can sleep you on plot seven, or for forty-five dollars we can upgrade you to plot twelve, directly under the moon."

Who in their lifetime, pre–Insomnia Crisis, could ever have imagined shelling out that kind of money to unroll a rubber mat in the dirt? But just hearing the soothing voices as they recite the Poppy Fields' menu of pricey sorceries is enough to implant these desires in me. Hungers appear in my mind, like coins flipped into a wishing pool.

America's great talent, I think, is to generate desires that would never have occurred, natively, to a body like mine, and to make those desires so painfully real that money becomes a fiction, an imaginary means to some concrete end. *Forty-five dollars for the moon-plot? Put it on the card. What a steal.*

"No," says Mr. Harkonnen. "You know what? No, thanks, miss."

He grabs my arm and then we're hurrying away. Red poppies lisp after us; if their magic works, we must be resistant to it. Neither of us keel over into slumber. We have to walk through these sections of the Poppy Fields with great care, because the shapes humping the grass are people.

Maybe ten minutes beyond the Poppy Fields, when the "enchanted" flowers have ebbed back into scraggly, depopulated weeds, Mr. Harkonnen stops to rub his eyes on his sleeve. "Too many people there tonight." His shoulders punch up at the sky angrily. "No privacy. Even if we paid the big money, I figured there would be some watcher there, lying a row away from us."

But that is not our problem any longer. Currently, we are moving parallel to the woods. There are a million visible stars, miles of dark. We seem to be the only two people.

Why did you bring me here? I do not ask him.

Abby—Baby A—she's a hero, I do not reassure him.

Instead I say:

"Mr. Harkonnen—Felix—do you think the elective insomniacs have a choice?"

He grunts, picking his way across the unlit grass.

"Yes. Some of them go to the hospital for help, and some come here to die."

"Do you think I gave you a choice?"

"Who do you think you are, girl? We chose. We're choosing. Only you assholes sure rigged the game up good. Now, if you hadn't shown up at our door in the first place . . . but let's walk."

We wander off into the shadows far beyond the ALL SORE-EYES WELCOME! sign, through uncut grass that brushes at my bare ankles; his hand drops to the small of my back, I take his arm, we are stumbling. All of this proceeds with a sultry inevitability, with a logic that mimics the odd chordal progressions of dreams, and for the first time in a long while I feel utterly relaxed. He frog-marches me far beyond the fairgrounds until I let him see that I'm not going to stumble; then he loosens his grip. Still he doesn't let go of my arm. Wherever we are now, we've missed the dividing line that separates the fairgrounds' unkempt margins from the nature preserve. Together we ford rivers of cattails, until the fever pitch of the Night World is entirely erased by distance, silence. The only sound is the occasional scream of some nocturnal hawk, which rips through the deep quiet of the sky like a skunk stripe drawn through black fur. We clamber over several enormous logs, Mr. Harkonnen grunting and slipping, offering me a hand. In the dark, these felled trees look as frighteningly misplaced as the bodies "sleeping" in the Poppy Fields. They make a lateral map of the woods as it must have been, before some storm. At one point, I look up and I see a spreading V pushing over the pines, many dozens of wings pulsing far above our heads; only it must be a very odd flock, because no shape resembles any other. Their wingspans, too, are irregular, some short and some long. Gaping up, I watch them multiply. What sort of flock is this, by what logic are so many different birds gathering? It's too dark to even guess at their names. Silvery light seems to pour from their wings, although I know this watershed must be an illusion caused by the mediating stars. Starlight liquefies and streams as the black shapes cross the Pleiades. They arrow over the trees so swiftly that before I can point out their bladed and scissoring bodies to Mr. Harkonnen, they are gone.

At last, when I am swaying on my feet, he stops.

"Here."

"Here's good. Sure."

"Now, lie down."

Overhead, two hawks carousel around. It's years since I've been this close to the green perfume of any woods.

"Stay put. No—Jesus, knock that off." He rolls his eyes. "Are you stupid? That's not why I brought you here."

I misunderstood. I assumed he needed a transfusion of something straightforward, something on the level of what I did with Jeremy. I rebutton my blouse.

Mr. Harkonnen lies down in the grass beside me, grunting.

Then he maneuvers my head onto his chest, makes a vise of his bicep. I cry out from surprise, just once, and a tawny blur streaks out of the scrub and runs past my cheek in the dirt. It's the fastest mouse in the world, I think, and then realize that my eyes are streaming.

"Here——" he repeats, trying to crook an arm under my shoulder. My hair gets yanked loose from its ponytail and spills onto his T-shirt. He shifts us around until my earlobe is pressed against the bony plate of his clavicle, where I can hear his heart drumming.

"Sleep!" he commands.

"Okay. Okay." I take a shuddery breath. "Why?"

"Because I said so," he says, viscous and triumphant. From his slur, I can hear how the medicines are dragging him under, too.

"You sleep for as long as I say, got it?"

"I will, Mr. Harkonnen."

This agreement is easy to broker. Nothing troubles me at all now.

"Good." He faces me on the grass, eye to eye under the pillow-white moon. "Night."

. . .

The following dawn with Baby A's father is one of the strangest of my life. How a person who so evidently hated me for months can now relate to me with such natural solicitousness is as bewildering as any flower opening in the desert. Whatever waters fed the blossoming of this affection are invisible to me. It's got to be some misdirection of the profoundest kind. Misplaced tenderness for Baby A, maybe, or for his wife, Justine. I wake up to a gray-flying sky, the sun not yet risen, and Mr. Harkonnen offering me a sip of water from his canteen. He takes the corner of his shirt, moist with dew, and rubs the dirt from my face.

I receive this kindness as best I can.

It's strange to see Mr. Harkonnen in daylight. We are our sober selves again, thank God. Dori, her memory, is caged as pressure in my ribs. Whatever came unraveled last night feels neatly spooled this morning. I exhale, feeling safer and safer as the sun inches up.

"How did you sleep?" he whispers.

"I slept beautifully. Thank you. And you?"

"I slept good," he grunts, suddenly bashful. "That lime stuff was killer, whatever we were drinking. I feel well rested."

"Did you dream?"

"If I did, I don't remember."

"Me neither."

Mr. Harkonnen nods, as if this is the bridge he's been waiting for.

He tells me he has a proposition for me, regarding dreams.

"I want you to make me a promise," he says. "Let's draw up a contract, right here. If you are going to continue to draw sleep from my daughter? I want you to swear that you'll give exactly that amount, every time. A matching donation. For as long as she gives, you give, too. You don't rest again until I say you can."

The sun shakes loose of the distant pines.

"Of course," I hear myself say.

We shake on this.

He nods twice, flushed and seemingly satisfied. With my free hand I peel a blade of grass from his stubbled chin. I find that I'm exhilarated by our contract's terms.

We stand up in the dirt. We laugh a little, to drain a pus

of awkwardness. I feel the strangest happiness. Tight muscles spasm everywhere in my arms, and an alkaline taste I can't name coats my throat. Mr. Harkonnen swallows. He has not released my palm.

Then I wish for whatever is flowing between us to remain unnamed, formless, unmeted into story or ever "experienced" in the past tense, and so concluded. I don't want to say it, I don't even want to try to understand it, and so begin to mistake it for something else, and something else after that, paling shadows of this original feeling, something inaudibly delicate that would not survive the passage into speech.

Shadows windmill over Felix's face. Like he's been caught out, suddenly, in some extradimensional autumn. Where are the falling leaves coming from? Clouds go racing over the field. Down below, our hands are still clasped. I'm relieved, relieved. I don't feel like a slave to the contract. I don't feel that Mr. Harkonnen tricked or frightened me into it. Each time I stare down at our handshake, I feel the same vertigo, a dislocation that is much stranger than mere anticipation, as though I'm being catapulted forward in time, rocketed to my death, perhaps, or to some absolute horizon, where I get a glimpse of my own life massing into form, and a thrilling feel for all that will happen to me now, all that I cannot know, haven't yet done, haven't spoken, haven't thought, will or won't. Just entering the contract does this. No matter what happens next, I'll have one constant now, won't I? Thanks to Felix, my dreams will be twinned to the dreams of his baby. The simple algebra of our arrangement feels like a ladder that he is holding out to me.

"I will not let you down," I tell Mr. Harkonnen. "I won't quit."

He gives me a tight smile, a look I recognize from my own mirror as the winched contentment of a recruiter; the pitch is finished, the contract inked and underway.

"All right. Better get us home."

Overhead, the sun is fully risen. A flock goes rowing over the pines, and this species I do recognize: they are Pennsylvania starlings. A hundred common gray-black birds, frequent visitors to our childhood backyard. They go shearing through the goggled blues of the May sky, the azure pools of air between the white clouds, moving east, each bird uniformly lit by the round sun. We walk under them, retracing our steps. Eventually Mr. Harkonnen drops my hand, but the world we return through feels solid and good.

. . .

Mr. Harkonnen drops me off a block from the Mobi-Office; I'm afraid my colleagues will recognize his brown and turquoise sedan and get the wrong impression. We did spend the night together, but that true statement is so misleading that I think it's worse than a lie. It's 7:02 a.m. But I see that as early as I am, I'm still not the first staffer to punch in.

JIM

....

"**H**ey," says Jim.

"Hello," I say.

DONOR Y

The Tuesday following my strange dawning with Mr. Harkonnen, an alert calls every staffer into the trailer. We fish-gape around Rudy's computer. Headquarters does a live broadcast from the DC offices, so that we learn about the Chinese orexins and electives fractionally faster than the rest of America.

Breaking news: several dozen patients suffering from the orexin-disruption have sought treatment at the Sanya Hospital in Hainan Province, China. This medical milestone delivers a quiet shock to all of us in the Mobi-Van. Naively, we now realize, we believed the dysfunction was bounded by our hemisphere, peculiar to American sleepers. But here is proof that nobody is quarantined by geography—that anybody, anywhere, might become an orexin.

It gets worse.

Fourteen Chinese insomniacs in the Hainan Province have also tested positive for the Donor Y nightmare. These people received sleep transfusions from an unknown source. The Corps was unaware of the existence of Chinese sleep clinics offering REM transfusions for cash. Initial reports suggest that the fourteen Chinese men and women infected with the Donor Y prion now exhibit an "extreme sleep aversion" similar to what we've seen with American elective insomniacs.

Presently, our doctors know so little about how the nightmare is spreading that they can only describe symptoms, guess at causes. But it's clear that my assurances were wrong. His dream is unchained, hopping bodies. The nightmare contagion is uncontained.

. . .

Jim calls me into his office.

"Are you avoiding me, Trish?"

"Ha-ha. That would be a ninja feat, wouldn't it, Jim? Avoiding you in this trailer."

"We barely speak."

I touch my throat, as if to suggest I have a common cold. At the same time, I feel this to be an accusatory gesture; Jim must know, of course, that his secret is the obstruction.

"Who are you talking to these days? I wonder."

But then the door comes unhinged; Rudy steps in.

In the narrow trailer window, I watch our faces darken like loaves in an oven.

"Huh," he says mildly. "Am I interrupting something?"

"I'm talking to Trish. As per our discussion."

"Oh. Right. We don't think it's a good idea for you to spend quite so much time with Baby A's family."

"It's just not professional . . ."

"Or it's *too* professional. They don't need that much from you, Edgewater."

"Your talents are now needed elsewhere."

"With the insomnia appearing on every continent . . ."

"With the nightmare-infection spreading . . ."

"Globally, we're going to have new initiatives, new responsibilities . . ."

The happiness spreads through me like a sickness I can't stop. I feel myself go fully automatic. A smile swarms onto my face, and somehow I am nodding at the brothers, taking notes. For a second it feels like old times to me, to stand under the headlamps of the brothers' concern. Not just for me, but for the entire planet; listening to them rant about the world in peril has always given me the most unlikely sense of security, made me feel like I am safely in the center of a rapidly enlarging family. And I think back to the night three weeks ago when I stood between Justine and Felix Harkonnen, staring through the glass into Ward Seven.

"I feel responsible for them," I say, staring from Jim to Rudy. "The Harkonnens."

"You'd better get over that," Rudy says. "You're not."

BABY A

....

Baby, baby. We're in a pickle now, aren't we, baby?

"Hush, hush," I murmur, bouncing her around the van.

It feels as if we're orbiting the same black hole. Her sleep will not stop flooding through her, shadowing her blood. My sister's ghost regenerates as one lean memory—the final hospital scene keeps doubling back on itself, repeating. So far, I've been diligent about making the matching donations. Many nights now, Baby A and I are going under sedation in tandem. Yesterday evening, for example, Nurse Carmen drew five hours from Abby in the Sleep Van, and I gave five hours at the bank.

Mrs. Harkonnen now refuses to let anybody but me touch her baby before the procedure begins. Thank God, there's not much to the prep—just rocking her to sleep, the basic bob-and-shush, the lullaby-bounce-step, that Dori and I perfected when we babysat in middle school. The nurses sterilize the helmet, spin-dry the soft cloth of the face mask. We hook the little bellows of her lungs to the larger bellows of our need.

They really do trust me now, Mr. and Mrs. Harkonnen. Somehow, I passed their independent screenings. They think I am sincere.

Another influx of misplaced faith that I must queasily endure, and assimilate into my body, for the greater good, says Rudy, who does pay attention, and who has noticed how my cheeks flame around Jim.

In a fairy tale, I would take Mrs. Harkonnen aside, suggest a scheme to deliver her daughter from our gloved hands, some prudent metamorphosis: We'll smuggle her out as a bear cub, a red rose, an eagle. We'll find some magical pair of shears to free your girl, I'd promise her. We'll cut you loose from the messy rest of us.

Instead, I show them our latest promotional video. It's genuinely uplifting—testimonials from survivors who've received their daughter's sleep transfusion. You can tell from the flat surf of each voice that a wave within them has crested and broken, and they are now safe on some far shore:

"The nightmare is over."

"The nightmare is over."

"It was a miracle: I slept through the night, and I woke up."

We three watch it together in the Harkonnens' living room, violin music swelling out of the speakers. Inside the Sleep Van, the video's hero, Baby A, snores lightly under the leaf-size green mask to replenish the black tanks of sleep.

Nurse Carmen knocks once and pops her head in: "She's done! Did a great job."

We switch the TV off.

Baby A goes back to her mom. Now she's awake and hungrily nursing, her white-socked feet doodling on air. One day soon she'll wake up to what we've done, and what we've taken from her.

"See you next Wednesday night."

"See you then," the two adult Harkonnens echo.

"We will never overdraw your daughter," I hear myself promise them, responding to some fleeting shadow that crosses both faces.

I make this promise at a moment when people are plunging their straws into any available centimeter of shale and water, every crude oil and uranium and mineral well on Earth, with an indiscriminate and borderless appetite. Fresh air, the sight of trees—these are birthrights and pleasures that we seem bent on extinguishing. Some animals we've turned out to be. We have never in our species' history respected Nature's limits, the doomsday speculators announce, smacking their lips, until it seems like some compensatory sucrose must flood into their mouths every time they say the words *mass death*. According to their estimates, our species will be extinct in another four generations, having exhausted every store of water and fuel on the planet. But this baby is small enough, and our need is great enough, that the nurses can be exquisitely precise, never withdrawing from her fleshy aquifer more than the recharge rate. We take, at most, six hours from her. We ration our greed.

The Sleep Van, that white pod, readies itself to pull away from the mothership of the Harkonnen residence.

"How far away are we from . . . from synthesis?" Mrs. Harkonnen wants to know.

"Oh, goodness. That's the dream, isn't it?"

Now we three give each other these faith transfusions.

Later, alone in the trailer, I continue to make outreach calls to donors with the narcotized zeal of all the other night-shift Corps recruiters: "Thanks to your generous support, eighteen insomniacs will sleep through the night, and open their eyes at dawn. Thirty-three percent of our patients make a full recovery."

You can't argue with those numbers, can you? I plan to one day ask Abigail.

Granted, we never gave you a choice, but wouldn't you have agreed to give those dreams to us, knowing now what you could not know then? This sort of subjunctive calculus, nobody teaches in school. Artificial sleep, for example, "sleep for all"— who can say if we will achieve it? I keep roto-dialing strangers, begging for their surplus unconsciousness. Next Wednesday night, Baby A and I are both scheduled to donate.

DORI

....

Ever since the dawn with Mr. Harkonnen, I have been unable to pitch in the same way. I have no idea why this should be so. I only know that at drives, I speak in my own voice about the Slumber Corps, and I don't retell the story of Dori's death. I don't relive her ending, or go into the convulsions. When my voice shakes, it's only because I'm nervous—I've got no practice at this sort of storytelling. I do talk about my sister, who she was before the crisis, although I find this makes me shy. Unfettered from her death, Dori's ghost takes on new shapes, and I find myself remembering more and more about her. In this new pitch, I describe her as a teenager, and even earlier. I mention the many insomniacs my sister's age or younger who have been cured by transfusions, and who can dream on their own once more thanks to the Slumber Corps. Often, I lead with Baby A. Imagine, I tell them, how she'll feel when she grows up, and learns how many lives she's saved.

If potential donors tell me they cannot afford to spare their sleep, I never press. The results of the new approach? By every metric we've got—donors recruited, sleep donated, insomniacs' lives saved—my pitch is a disaster. There are drives where I only recruit five donors. There was one drive, on a rainy Thursday night outside the shopping mall, where I recruited none. My "zeros" were actually zero, which has never happened to me before. I've fallen so far that I'm not even ranked, nationally, as a recruiter. In our Solar Zone, I'm number three of six. But you know what? Some people do give. I'll leave a Sleep Drive with a third fewer recruits than I was expecting for a crowd that size, but Dori, inside the people with whom I leave her story, is an ellipsis, alive. She's not a nightmare I've implanted within them—of that much, I feel almost certain.

. . .

If I stop telling Dori as a story, I wonder, where will she go?

. . .

Jim's out-and-out despondent. He paces our trailer with watering eyes. It's that Jim-despair that feels at once completely false, like the maudlin dirges of horn instruments on a Mexican soap, and authentically out of his control. Rudy Storch is furious with me, salty and affronted; worse yet, I'll sometimes catch him casting me looks of feral betrayal, as if somehow I'm the toothy trap that sprang shut on his paw.

"Edgewater, goddammit. Have you seen your zeros? How you sleep at night, I do not know. This experiment is *up*; it has got to stop."

He grits his teeth; he doesn't touch me now or scream at me. He won't joke.

"Please. Please. I understand that *you're* more comfortable. But what you're doing is irresponsible. It's . . . it's . . ." he'd sputtered, his eyes cloudy with exhaustion. "It's . . ."

He never finishes, and it doesn't matter. Dori's escaped from the grammar of the horror story I've been telling about her. Her ghost has quieted, become uncooperative. I can't go back to the old style of pitching now.

THE WHISTLEBLOWER'S HOTLINE

The first three times I call, I hang up.

The fourth time I call, I get an automated female voice, thanking me for contacting the Slumber Corps Whistleblower's Program. This unshockable voice instructs me to leave the most detailed message possible about the institutional corruption I have witnessed, or in which I have participated, to include fraud, waste, abuse, policy violations, discrimination, illegal conduct, unethical conduct, unsafe conduct, or any other misconduct by the Slumber Corps organization, its employees or its volunteers.

I drop the phone as if scalded.

. . .

To honor my contract with Mr. Harkonnen, I take the bus to make my donation at our regional Sleep Donation Station. This month I am certain that I will be rejected at the screening—I have been dreaming of Baby A nonstop, of the flutter-suck of her tiny mouth. In one nightmare, she breastfed from my sister, who had a saint's face in death, pale and sad and lit strangely from below, one green eye eaten away.

What uglier proof of its deep pollution could my mind present me with?

I am afraid of these dreams, which I cannot stop or change.

I am afraid that even my desire to do good will spin out of my control and become evil.

Orexins have been reported in Uganda, Taiwan, England. Infected sleep was transfused in Chile. In the Mobi-Office, Jim is calling me "baby" again, I think because it's been a month now and I haven't said anything to anyone about Baby A's exported sleep. Sometimes I think I can feel Jim's secret exerting a subtle gravity in my body, like a sick second pulse. I worry that it's warping my dreams in ways their machines won't uncover in time and perverting even my conscious intentions.

At the reception window, I clear my throat.

"I think my sleep might be unusable this week, miss. I think there is something wrong with it."

To which an icy voice replies, "Have a seat. We'll be the judge of that."

And I wonder: How many of the donors seated around me are secretly hoping for a similar outcome? To be exposed as broken, corrupted—to have our impurities discovered, under some investigator's microscope, so that we can be exempted from ever having to give again? "Opting out"—Jim's grim euphemism seems to apply here, too. What a relief, I think, to never again worry that you might be the one poisoning the nation's sleep supply. Is anybody else having this fantasy with me? I gaze around the waiting room, where six of us are waiting to learn if our dreams are healthy. One robust lady in a Minnie Mouse sweatshirt is scribbling furiously on her clipboard; she leans over to ask me, "Honey, how do you spell 'piranha'?"

There is something terribly funny to me about watching other donors holding their stubby number-two pencils, transcribing their dreams into flat grammar on real paper.

One night soon, I'm sure, the notion of self-reporting will seem unimaginably old-fashioned. The butter churn of data collection. Almost everything else we do and say is now recorded: what we read, what we purchase, what we whisper to one another near speakers. Easily, I can imagine a new generation of children who wire themselves to the great glowing mind of the Slumber Corps. Children who grow up with the expectation that their dreams will be monitored by others.

I've heard rumors that our Corps scientists are presently trying to develop a "sleep mask" that will upload live feeds of people's dreams into a global dream database. If that's true, it would be a very ambitious project—translating spikes of cerebral electricity into the faces and animals and nameless kingdoms that people see when they dream. A mask that would help the doctors to "nip a future nightmare contagion in the bud," as Jim told me, still smiling even after I pointed out that the bud in his metaphor was, somewhat distressingly, a human head. A "sleep mask" to map our secret lives—so secret, in some cases, that even we don't know about them. Perhaps soon it will become illegal to dream alone. What could be more dangerous?

Sitting in the freezing waiting room, watching donors filing behind the flimsy plastic curtains, I find it takes no effort to imagine a bleak future where people get pulled from their beds, arrested for failing to wear their state-issued "sleep mask." Jailed for doing their dreaming off-line, in the deep privacy of their bodies. Of course, the alternative is also terrifying:

Depending on the honor system of self-reporting. On human recall, human goodness. Look, I shudder at that prospect myself. What human wouldn't?

I find myself marveling at the courage of the staffers, smiling ordinary smiles as they take the questionnaires from us. Sometimes you can see the tremor of a warranted fear—is it safe to receive these descriptions? Is it possible that the wrong words might take root inside them, mutate their own dreams?

It takes some time to input my nightmare onto the form. Then I have to wait even longer for them to check my history against the known infectious nightmares. At the end of the hall, in custard-colored booths the size of library carrels, potential donors are going over their nightmares with staff members. I catch fragments:

". . . a bunny-like twitchy face . . ."

". . . and the barber had electric-green hair . . ."

"Okay!" says an administrator to her donor brightly. "You're good to go here, Donald!"

This is really it, I think. You are about to be banned from donation. Greedily, I start to hope for this. It's so sly, the way that fears and hopes and dreams and nightmares can belly-flip into one another. The longer I sit in the hard chair, the more I want to be dismissed. Fondly I recall excused absences and doctors' notes, those pink tickets to hours of solitude. Chicken pox, which I contracted at age ten and somehow never gave to Dori—that July quarantine returns to me now as a happy memory. One p.m. and the green-cheesecloth curtains drawn, the relief of seeing no one, doing nothing, scratching my sores in secret, breaking in my monster skin alone. *Exempt me, exempt me.* For reasons of public safety, for the greater good, tell me I can go home now and sleep for myself only.

"No," says the attending physician, "nothing here to disqualify you."

She gives me a wide, patient smile, as if to suggest that she deals with hypochondriacs like me hourly, people who believe that their nightmares must be uniquely wretched, worse than anybody else's, who fall for the body's shaky aggrandizements of its plans and pains.

I'm incredulous: "You're sure? You want to check the database again?"

It's not pure, she says, my sleep; but it's good enough, and the need is urgent.

"You're still eligible to give, Mrs. Edgewater."

So I do.

. . .

Summer greens the trees on 3300 Cedar Ridge Parkway, and I continue to donate. For every hour Baby A gives, I give my hour. But I have the queasy feeling without pause now; it seems there's nothing I can do that's not a betrayal of Dori, or of somebody's dead or breathing, conscious or sleeping, much-loved body.

DONOR Y

Breaking news: Donor Y has been discovered by the authorities. He flew into SFO from Oahu and was apprehended by a customs agent. His image is splashed everywhere. In his passport photo, Donor Y looks so ordinary: he's got a crew cut, a square jawline, brown eyes. All the obvious symmetries. Acne scars swirl over his cheeks like just-audible music. It's the kind of face that can be forgotten instantly, or easily digested into any crowd. From his bland expression, you would never assume this person could gestate and host the most virile, lethal nightmare in the world's history. His name has still not been released.

According to preliminary reports, this man claims he had no idea that he was infected with a nightmare at the time of his donation. He is pleading innocent to the charges that he deliberately sabotaged our nation's sleep supply. He agrees to a polygraph test and insists that he has never had the nightmare himself. He's been sleeping soundly, apparently, for months. So Donor Y may turn out to be exactly what I feared the most: a good soul. Another human capsule, as clueless as the rest of us about his mind's contents.

BABY A

....

"**P**lease help me," I say when she answers the door. "Is Felix home?"

"Trish!" she mouths silently. Pantomiming, which means the baby is sleeping.

"Oh dear, what's wrong? Don't worry."

She hugs me on the front porch, and I hug her back, for a length of time that would feel unnatural with anybody but Justine Harkonnen. I try to record, to preserve in my skeleton, in my muscle memory, exactly how this feels. I figure there's a real chance that thirty minutes from now I'll be back on the lawn. Ousted from the Harkonnens' lives for good, or even, it's occurred to me, in the back of a police car. If I were a gambling woman, I'd wager that I am about to be expelled from both my families—the Harkonnens, the Slumber Corps.

Felix must be home—the turquoise and brown car is baking in the sun. Strays weave around its tires like material shadows. There is a universe where I never tell the Harkonnens what I learned about Jim. Or how I tried to use my dead sister, like tongs, to get something supple and alive out of them. I rest my head on Justine's shoulder; instinctively, her hand flies up to pat my back. A driver in a passing car might think we are dancing in place. Through the doorway, I can see Mr. Harkonnen rocking Baby A, who is sleeping for herself this afternoon. Only her head pokes out of the yellow sling, which makes Abigail look like the crinkled face in the moon. Deep inside me, I feel Dori stirring, her dead eyes opening to peer out through mine. Dori, in life, was honest "to a fault," as they say. She's dead, I mostly believe that, but we all pray, don't we? To ourselves, if not to some provident Eye in the clouds.

In the doorframe, Mrs. Harkonnen is smiling, shining, with that innocence that we of the Slumber Corps love and abhor in her. With those wide-sky eyes, all blue, and a faith in me that I will never comprehend, Mrs. Harkonnen ushers me into her home. She says in a whisper, so as not to wake her baby daughter, "Come in, Trish. Whatever's wrong, we'll get to the bottom of it. I'm sure we can figure this out."

THE WHISTLEBLOWER'S HOTLINE

The good news, or the mixed news, it might be fairer to say, is that I will not be performing this information transfusion for the first time.

Last night, I called the hotline. Actually, I called the hotline about a hundred times. I couldn't speak, and I couldn't speak, I lost track of how many times I dropped the call, and then the seventieth or the eleven-hundredth time that I dialed this hotline, for no reason I was able to discern, I heard myself begin.

After the phone clicked down, I woke up to what I'd done.

Questions I held at bay for the call's duration flooded into me then, as if I'd floated back within range of a radio tower. What if all donations dry up after the Corps scandal breaks, and more people suffer? What if Jim is a good man, a good thief, doing something "ugly but necessary," as he told me—accelerating the science that will lead to a cure—and I've just made a horribly shortsighted mistake? But I find another theory far more plausible—that Jim's plan was never to unlock the cure for the

Insomnia Crisis, but to fill his own pockets. Perhaps the Corps' shadow objective has always been to create "new global markets" for the most precious commodity of our time. And this is the scenario that closes my throat.

Blink to blink, I toggled between these grandiose, apocalyptic fears to visions of a tiny infant in her crib, breathing.

I slumped, cored and cold, the way I used to feel after drives. I sat watching the gray phone where it levitated on the wall, but no human from the Ethics & Compliance office called me back. I wonder who picks up these messages.

All that dial tone I ingested must have come roaring out of me. To get the whole story across properly, with all its nuances, I had to call back several times, resuming where I'd left off. When I finished, the scraped white moon was out. Near the end of my transmission, I heard myself, insanely, thanking the chittering machine for recording so much tape, and I felt a quaky relief, thinking that at last I was rid of it, that events would now rush to meet us, but at least I'd been honest, or as honest as I could be, starting with my first association with the Harkonnens. I leaned my head against the wall, listening to the droning silence. I exhausted myself with speculations about whether I'd set the wrong or the right outcome in motion. Unsurprisingly, last night I couldn't sleep. I wondered what, if anything, would happen as a result of the phone call—if even now some dream or nightmare was massing into our future, gathering like weather, becoming real. But I also thought, with the sly old happiness, *No matter what tomorrow brings, you can be sure of at least one thing, Edgewater: tonight you've given Dori's story to a stranger.*

ACKNOWLEDGMENTS

This novella was originally published as a digital-only ebook in 2014 by the now-shuttered Atavist Books. It was a bold experiment and I am honored to have been a part of it. Thank you to the wonderful Frances Coady and the Atavist Books team.

I'm so happy that *Sleep Donation* is now available in this gorgeously designed and illustrated edition from Vintage Books. My enormous gratitude to Denise Shannon, Jordan Pavlin, Gail Gaynin, Kayla Overbey, Linda Huang, Christopher Zucker and Debbie Glasserman, Andy Hughes, Barbara Richard, Robin Witkin, Rima Weinberg, Kathy Strickman, Angie Venezia, and Laura Chamberlain.

Thank you, Anna Kaufman, for giving this book its second life. I'm so grateful for your keen editorial eye and for the serious consideration you gave to even the wildest material.

Thanks to Stephen King, for his early and continued support.

Thank you to Ale + Ale, for your nightmarish and hauntingly beautiful artwork.

Thanks to my children, Oscar and Ada, for the free home lessons in the horrors of sleep deprivation.

And thank you all for reading it.

ACTIVE NIGHTMARE OUTBREAKS IN THE U.S.

PROTECT YOURSELF AND OTHERS!

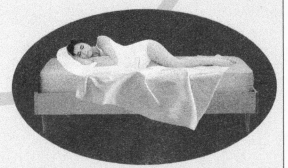

A dream is the most honest communication a body can have with itself. Now we are depending on you to be honest about your symptoms.

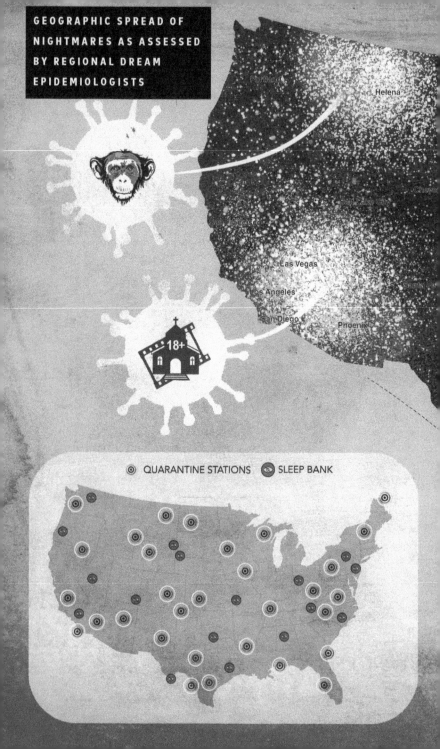

GEOGRAPHIC SPREAD OF
NIGHTMARES AS ASSESSED
BY REGIONAL DREAM
EPIDEMIOLOGISTS

QUARANTINE STATIONS   SLEEP BANK

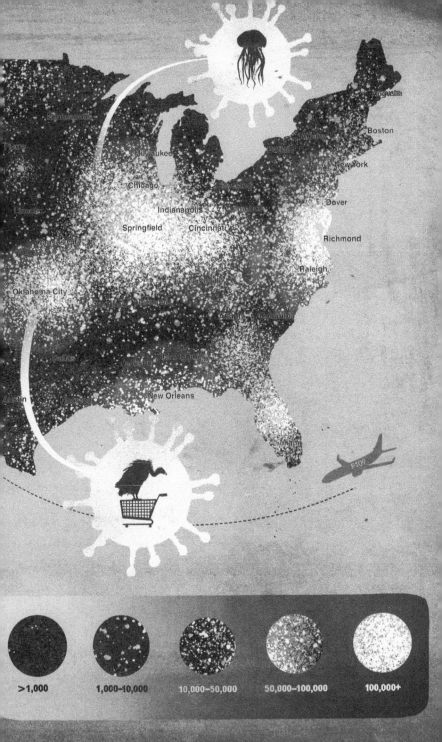

Augusta

Albany
Buffalo
New York

Dover

Richmond

Raleigh

Columbia

Boston

Minneapolis

Pierre

Milwaukee

Chicago

Cleveland

Indianapolis

Columbus

Lincoln

Springfield

Cincinnati

Kansas City

Nashville

Oklahoma City

Little Rock

Memphis

Atlanta

Dallas

Jackson

Montgomery

Austin

Houston

New Orleans

Miami

F100

>1,000   1,000–10,000   10,000–50,000   50,000–100,000   100,000+

Report to the nearest quarantine station immediately if your dream contains one or more of the following images:

THE DREAM OF A FRESH HUMILIATION

ACTIVE OUTBREAK

MOST VIRULENT STRAIN

Your Sex Tape Screening in the Old Cathedral

NIGHTMARE CLUSTERS REPORTED IN AZ, CA, NM, NV, UT

LESS COMMON STRAINS

- Wallpaper made of your poor report cards
- Your name misspelled on the headstone
- Surgeons snipping at the overgrown vines in your belly
- Your wolfhound leaving you for the neighbor man
- Winning a tank of naked hermit crabs

THE DREAM OF THE GAZE YOU'VE BEEN AVOIDING

ACTIVE OUTBREAK

MOST VIRULENT STRAIN

Monkeys' Faces Hiding in the Roses

NIGHTMARE CLUSTERS REPORTED ID, MT, WY

LESS COMMON STRAINS

- Ex-lovers' portraits on a deck of playing cards
- Six wattled turkeys assessing you from the jury box
- Your daughter's black eye pressed against the submarine porthole
- Unzipping a body bag and staring into your own blue face

NEW PLAGUE DREAMS OF THE MIDDLE WEST

MOST VIRULENT STRAIN

Vultures in the Deserted Supermarket Aisles

NIGHTMARE CLUSTERS REPORTED IN IA, IL, KS, MO, NE, OK

LESS COMMON STRAINS

- Prehistoric grasshoppers fiddling on truck hoods
- Aurochs grazing on your linens at the laundromat
- Heavy rains of jackrabbits, hind legs drumming on rooftops
- Giant fixed-wing dragonflies idling on the tarmac
- Tiny gray frogs pouring out of showerheads and kitchen taps
- Miniature bears infesting the trees
- Matchstick pronghorns racing over tabletops

THE DREAM OF THE JELLYFISH ATTACK

MOST VIRULENT STRAIN

Meteor Shower of Jellyfish Stingers

NIGHTMARE CLUSTERS REPORTED IN FL, GA, IL, NC, OH, SC, VA

LESS COMMON STRAINS

- Wedding tents with writhing white tentacles
- Baseball playoffs canceled for inclement weather; Wrigley Field covered in livid bubbles
- Caribbean cruise-goers watching stingers sizzle onto the Lido Deck
- Screaming children carried off by jellyfish balloons

As the etiology and transmission dynamics of these nightmares have yet to be determined, the Slumber Corps recommends a cautious approach to all symptomatic dreamers

THE DREAM OF NO ESCAPE

- Airport where the departures board and the arrivals board are identical, i.e., Cedar Rapids–Cedar Rapids
- Motorcycle handlebars replaced by snakes
- Gas pumps covered in black hoods
- Boxes of hundreds of rusting doorknobs
- Elevator suspended between worlds
- Scorpions curled around boot soles
- Windows hardening into mirrors
- Nursery furniture adrift on a melting glacier

THE UNRIPENING DREAM

- Ripe oranges slowly turning green again
- Old-growth forests shrinking into acorns
- Alligators filing backward into their eggs
- Ink leaking out of encyclopedias into clear puddles
- Renaissance portraits devolving into ultrasounds

THE NIGHTMARE OF THE WATERFALL OF CHILDREN'S TEETH

- Deep woods, red moon
- Hard glint of something that is not water
- Horror, horror, horror

THE NIGHTMARE OF THE HAUNTED JUKEBOX

- Whiskey glasses sparkling at each empty barstool
- Obituary photos on the album covers
- Voices of your cremated relations drifting through speakers
- Scratchy recording of a herd of extinct mammoths trumpeting
- Blue sparks around the unplugged electrical cord

THE NIGHTMARE OF THE FINAL EXAM

- Grade-school class holding conch shells to their ears
- No. 2 pencils gripped in pudgy fists, transcribing a roaring
- Substitute teacher in antique diving suit, clapping erasers
- Black water lapping at the school windows
- Ancient dial tone of the primordial ocean

THE DREAM WHERE YOU ARE THE CONTAMINATED DONOR

- Pandora's box emptied by pneumatic tubes
- Leprous bats hanging from your shoe tree
- Spiderwebs bridging your eyelids
- Your worst secret exhaled into the dream tanks
- Sick children murmuring your name

HELP US TO STOP A NIGHTMARE CONTAGION BEFORE IT BEGINS

PLEASE NOTE ALL RELEVANT SYMPTOMS IN YOUR DREAM JOURNALS AND IMME-DIATELY CALL THE NATIONAL NOTIFIABLE DREAM SURVEILLANCE SYSTEM

LET YOUR DOCTOR KNOW WITHOUT DELAY—

1. If you see one or more of the following colors in your dreams:

Coma white	Preschool fishbowl blue
Tarantula hair violet	Mortician's lipstick red
Rabbit's eye pink	Ghost rainbow
Molar yellow	Stampeding gray
Buick LeSabre on fire blue	Wolf's gumline purple
Smoker's Lung black	Famine brown
Corn maze green	Spat blood maroon
Hyena's laughter silver	Venusian orange

2. If you see these numbers in your dreams: 44, 1.618, 666, 1,492, –13, 4,141,912, 000,000,000,000.

3. If your dream features one or more of these sensations: wiggling a very loose tooth; tasting red clouds as you plummet earthward; growing a thin, forked tail from your coccyx bone; choking on seawater; kissing your best friend's long-dead mother.

4. If you engage in one or more of the following activities in a dream: falling in love with a postage stamp; eating a bucket of sour cherries; opening the small, green vault of a barrel

cactus; milking a reptile; gonging a clapperless bell; driving
an empty school bus; drawing winged bison on a cave wall;
winning a lottery that you do not recall entering; biting
down on a stranger's wedding band; riding a land tortoise;
manning a lighthouse; house-sitting for twin witches;
instigating an orgy under a Christmas tree; forgiving your
murderer; floating up into the early moon.

5. If you frequent one of these establishments in a dream:

Red Suds Laundromat	Samarra
Lucky Devil Strip Club	Daytona
Lady Feathers' Fried Chick-N	The Grand Cauldron
Uncle Bump's Go-Karts	The Bowl-a-Bed Hotel
Mount Nowhere	

6. If you hear one or more of the following sounds in a dream:
baritone chuckling; a buzz saw biting into a tree; giraffes humping;
an infant reciting Dante; choirs of owls; bad guitar solos; the ultra-
sonic howling of a falling star; a finger bone snapping; a widow spi-
der's footfalls; the scream of brakes failing; a child blowing out a
thousand candles; a music too beautiful for words

7. If you have a dream, even seemingly benign, that recurs
more than twice in a 72-hour period.

8. If you have *any dream* in which you observe yourself
sleeping, on a bed that is identical to your own, in a world
that is indistinguishable from this one, and you watch
yourself *beginning to wake up.*

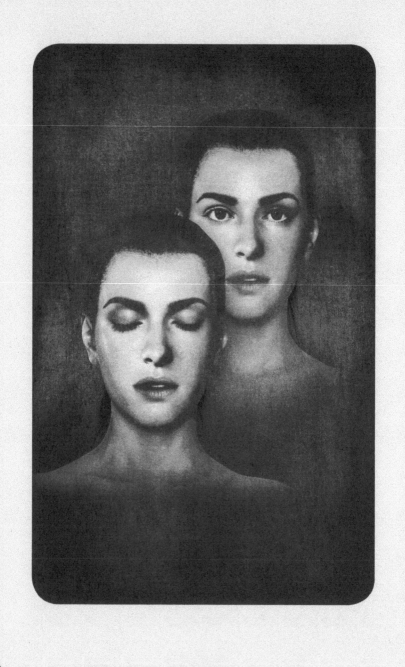